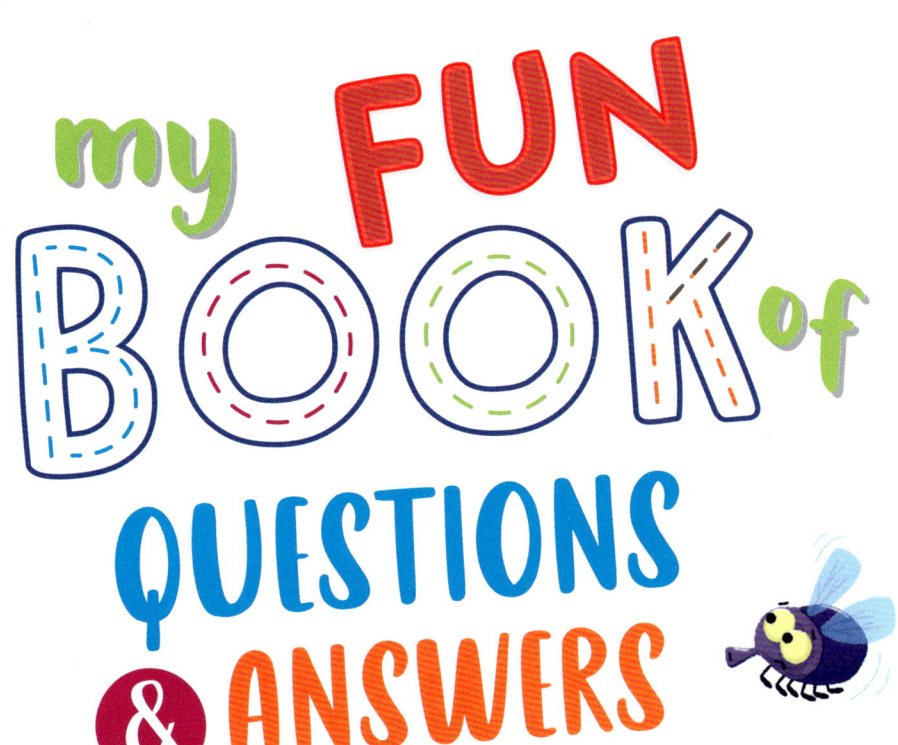

my FUN BOOK of QUESTIONS & ANSWERS

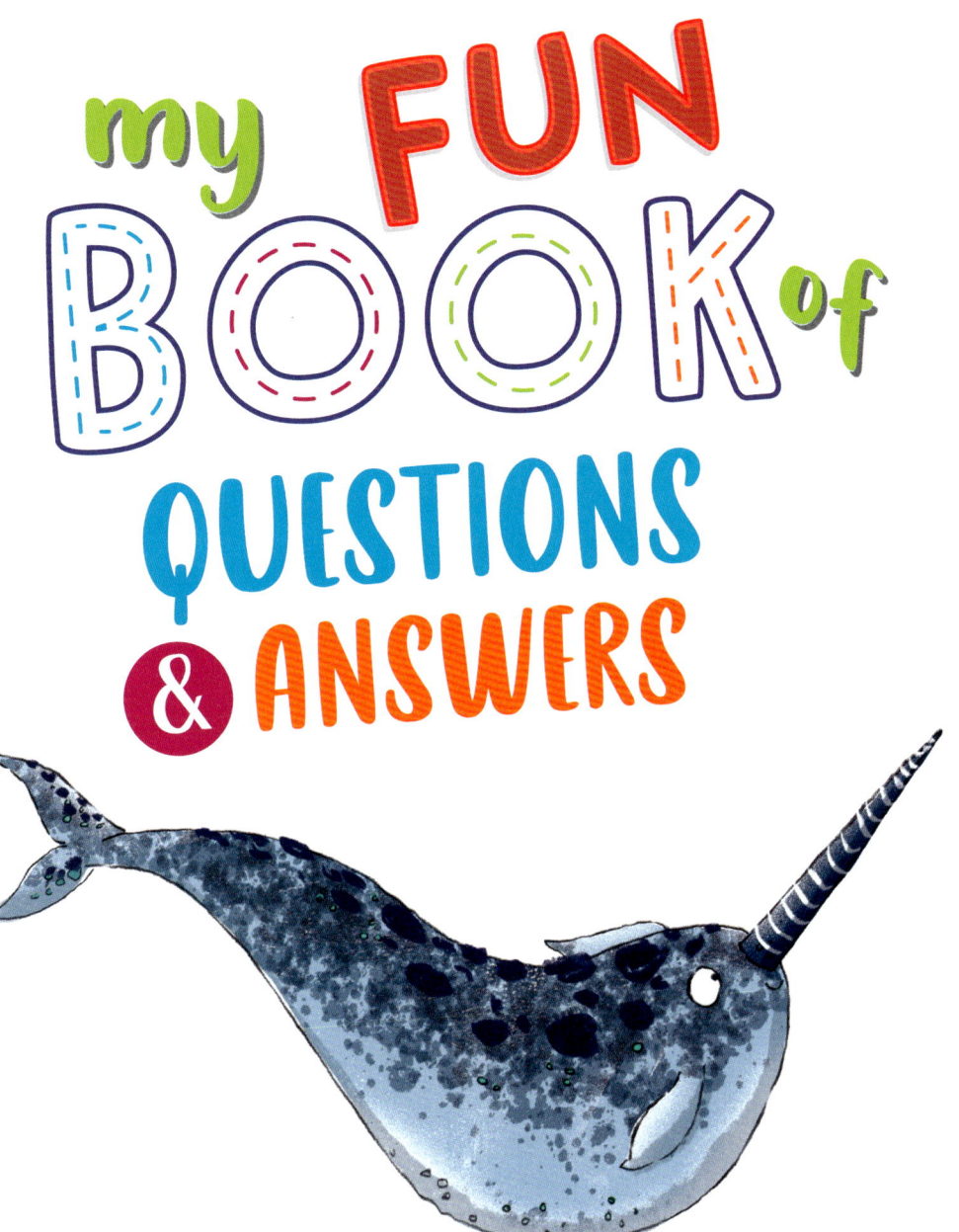

Little Hippo Books

First published in 2022 by Miles Kelly Publishing Ltd
Harding's Barn, Bardfield End Green, Thaxted, Essex, CM6 3PX, UK

Copyright © Miles Kelly Publishing Ltd 2022

2 4 6 8 10 9 7 5 3 1

Publishing Director Belinda Gallagher
Creative Director Jo Cowan
Editorial Director Rosie Neave
Senior Editors Sarah Carpenter, Claire Philip
Design Manager Joe Jones
Production Elizabeth Collins
Image Manager Liberty Newton
Reprographics Stephan Davis

All rights reserved. No part of this publication may be reproduced, stored in a retrieval system, or transmitted by any means, electronic, mechanical, photocopying, recording, or otherwise, without the prior permission of the copyright holder.

ISBN 978-1-960009-27-2

Printed in China

Made with paper from a sustainable forest

littlehippobooks.com

CONTENTS

Science 6

Human Body 18

Planet Earth 30

Oceans 44

Seashore 60

Plants 76

Rain Forests 90

Big Cats 106

Baby Animals 118

Monkeys and Apes 130

Deadly Creatures 144

Index 156

Is science in the playground?

Yes, it is! Lots of science happens in a playground. The playground rides could not work without science. A seesaw is a simple machine called a lever. It has a long arm and a point in the middle called a pivot. As you ride on the seesaw, the lever tips up and down on the pivot.

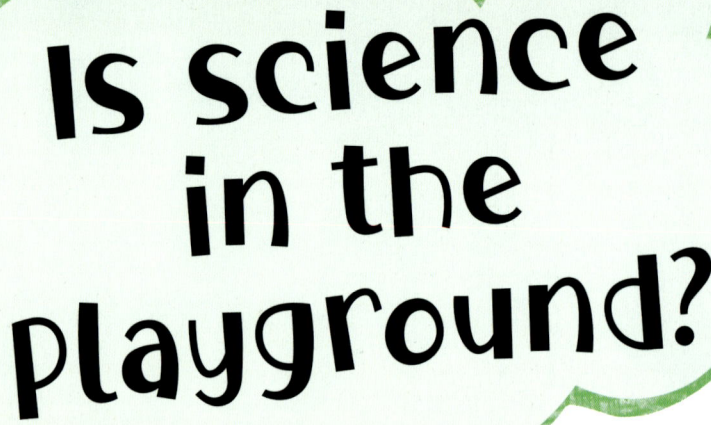

Lever

Pivot

Feel
Press your palm onto a table. A force called friction stops you sliding your hand along.

What is a wheel?

A wheel is a very simple machine that can spin around. Wheels let other machines, such as skateboards, bicycles, cars, and trains, roll along smoothly. They also make it easy to move heavy weights in carts and wheelbarrows.

Paralympic athlete

Roller coaster

Sloping machine

A ramp is the simplest machine of all. It is easier to walk up a ramp to the top of a hill than it is to climb a steep hillside.

What makes things stop and start?

Pushes and pulls make things stop and start. Scientists use the word "force" for pushes and pulls. Forces are all around us. The force of gravity pulls things downward. It makes a roller coaster car hurtle downhill. It also slows the car on the uphill parts of the track.

Why do fireworks flash and bang?

Fireworks flash and bang because they are full of chemicals that burn. The chemicals have lots of energy stored in them. When they burn, the energy changes to light, heat, and sound. We use chemicals that burn in other places too, such as stoves, heaters, and engines.

Fireworks

How do candles burn?

Candles are made of wax and a wick (string). When the wick is lit, the wax around it melts. The wick then soaks up the liquid wax and the heat of the flame turns the wax into a gas (vapor), which burns away. As the wax becomes vapor it cools the wick, allowing the candle to burn slowly.

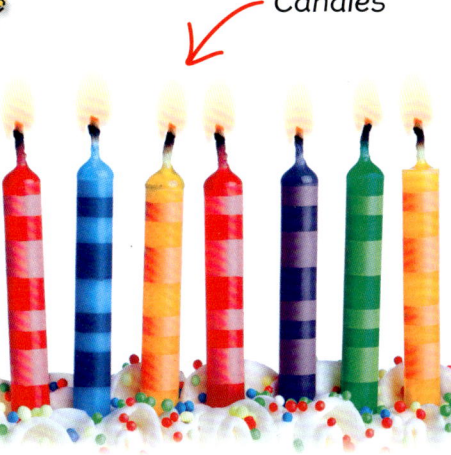

Candles

Hot! Hot! Hot!
The hottest temperature ever recorded was in a science laboratory. It was 720 million degrees Fahrenheit (720,000,000°F).

Remember
Which piece of equipment is used to measure how hot or cold something is?

Thermometer

What is a thermometer?

A thermometer is an instrument that measures temperature—how hot something is. The numbers on a thermometer may show the temperature in degrees Fahrenheit (°F). If you put a thermometer in ice water, it shows 32°F. If you put it in boiling water it shows 212°F. A thermometer can also measure body temperature.

How does light bend?

Light rays travel in straight lines. When light shines through a prism, the rays bend because light travels more slowly through glass than air. Sunlight is called white light, but it is made up of a mixture of colors. When white light passes through a prism it splits into many colors, like a rainbow.

Make
On a sunny day, stand with your back to the Sun. Spray water into the air and you should see a rainbow!

White light

Prism (glass triangle)

Fast as light
Light is the fastest thing in the Universe. It travels 186,000 miles every second. That means it could travel around the Earth seven times in less than a second!

What is the loudest sound?

The roar of a jet engine is the loudest sound we normally hear. It is thousands of times louder than someone shouting. Sounds this loud can damage our ears if we are too close to them.

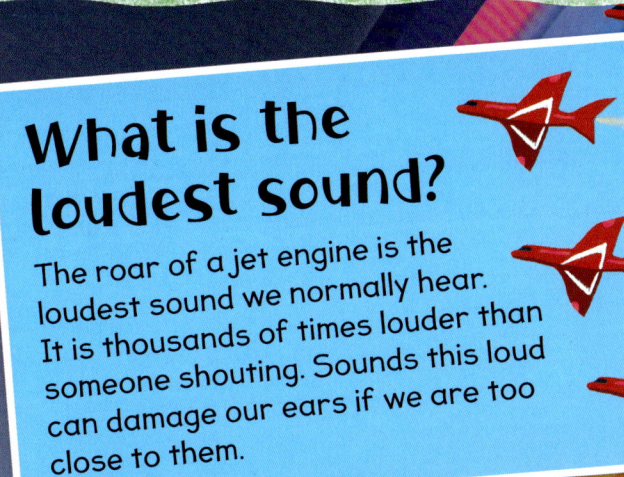

Jet aircraft

Rainbow colors

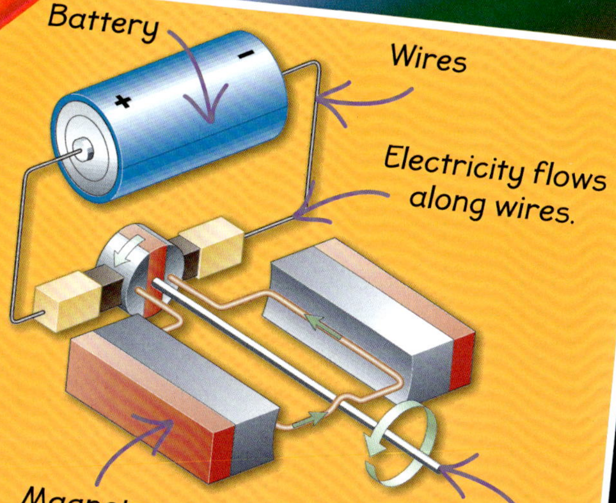

Battery

Wires

Electricity flows along wires.

Magnet on side of motor

Spindle

What is inside an electric motor?

Magnets and wires are inside an electric motor. Electricity from a battery passes through the wires, which turns the wires into a magnet. Two more magnets on each side of the motor push and pull against the wires. This makes a thin metal rod (spindle) spin around.

How do you make magnets?

By using another magnet. Magnets are made from lumps of iron or steel. You can turn a piece of iron into a magnet by stroking it with another magnet. A magnet can also be made by sending electricity through a coil of wire. This is called an electromagnet. Some electromagnets are so strong, they can pick up cars.

Magnet

Count
Find a magnet at home (you can use a fridge magnet). How many paper clips can your magnet pick up?

Does a magnet have a field?

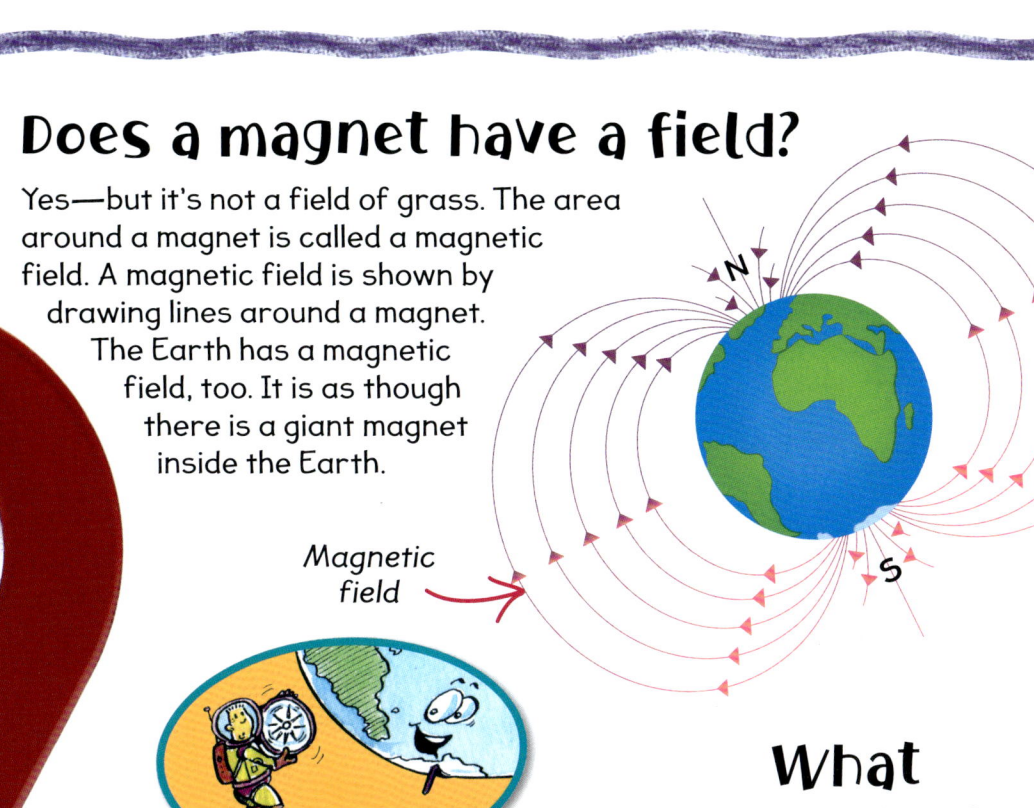

Yes—but it's not a field of grass. The area around a magnet is called a magnetic field. A magnetic field is shown by drawing lines around a magnet. The Earth has a magnetic field, too. It is as though there is a giant magnet inside the Earth.

Magnetic field

Handy rock

Some rocks act like magnets. Years ago, people used magnetic rocks to find their way. If they let the rock spin around, it always pointed in the same direction.

What are poles?

Every magnet has two poles. These are where the pull of a magnet is strongest. They are called the north pole and the south pole. A north pole and a south pole always pull toward each other. Two north poles always push each other away. So do two south poles.

Where does electricity come from?

Electricity comes to your home along cables from power plants. The cables are held off the ground by electricity pylons. Around your home are holes in the wall called sockets. When a machine is plugged into a socket, electricity flows out to work the machine.

Excellent electric

Our homes are full of machines that use a lot of electricity. If we didn't have access to electricity we wouldn't have televisions, lights, washing machines, or computers!

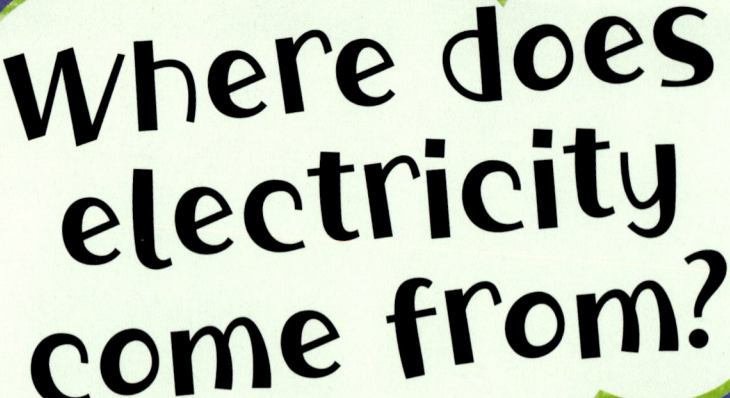

Power plant

Electricity pylon holds cables off the ground.

What is a circuit?

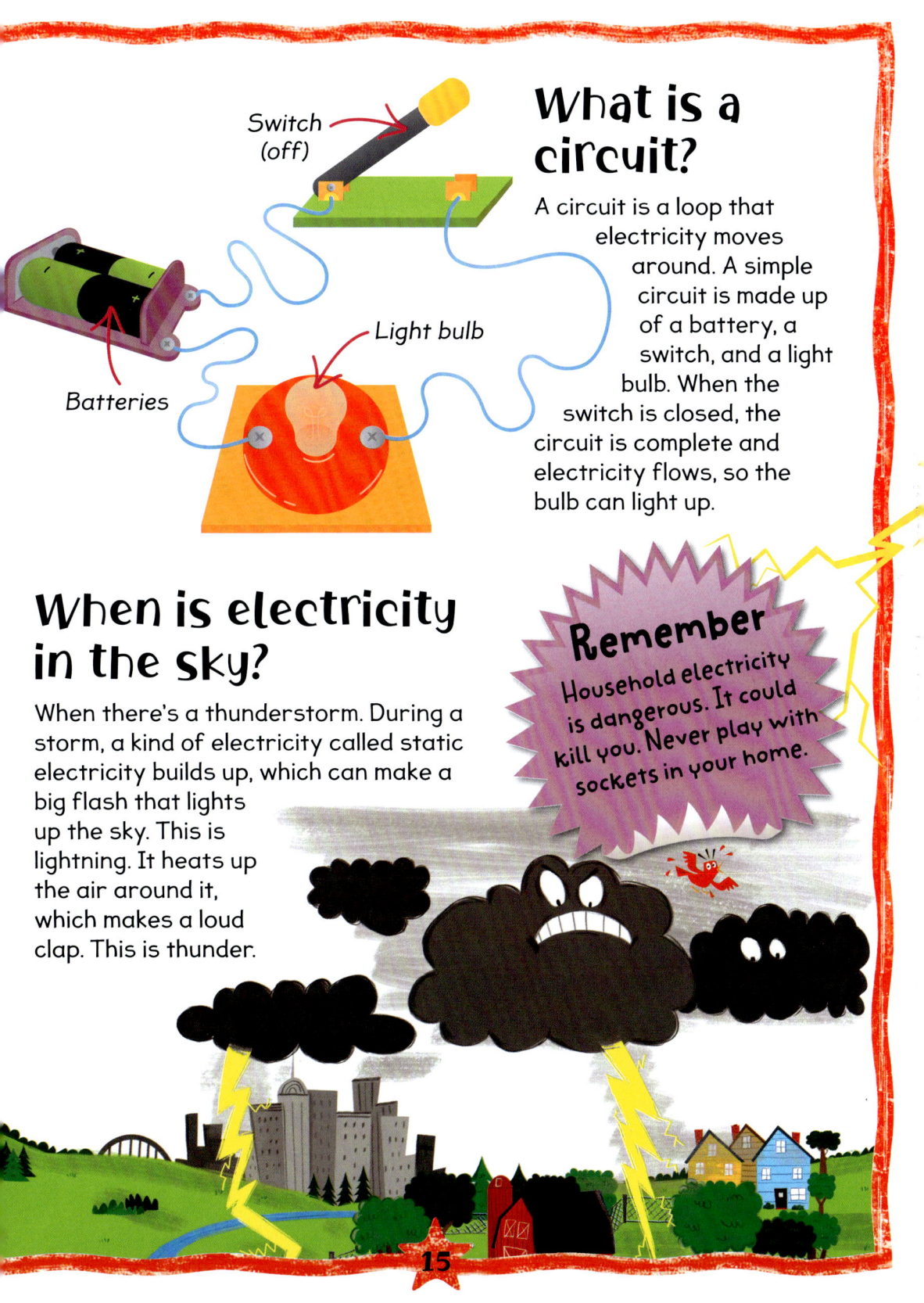

Switch (off)

Batteries

Light bulb

A circuit is a loop that electricity moves around. A simple circuit is made up of a battery, a switch, and a light bulb. When the switch is closed, the circuit is complete and electricity flows, so the bulb can light up.

When is electricity in the sky?

When there's a thunderstorm. During a storm, a kind of electricity called static electricity builds up, which can make a big flash that lights up the sky. This is lightning. It heats up the air around it, which makes a loud clap. This is thunder.

Remember

Household electricity is dangerous. It could kill you. Never play with sockets in your home.

How is the Internet like a web?

The Internet is made up of millions of computers around the world. They are connected like a giant spider's web! A computer connects to a machine called a modem. This sends signals to a server. The server lets you connect to the Internet. People can send emails and open web pages.

What does www stand for?

The letters www are short for World Wide Web. The World Wide Web is like a giant library of information, stored on computers all over the world. There are also millions of stores on the World Wide Web, where you can buy almost anything.

Find out

With a grown-up, use the Internet to find out who invented the World Wide Web.

The world is connected by the Internet.

Computer room

The first computer was made 70 years ago. It was so big that it filled a whole room and weighed around 55 tons.

Can I use the Internet without a computer?

Yes. Other machines like cell phones can link to the Internet, so you can find out information and send and receive emails too. A cell phone connects to the Internet by radio.

What does my skin do?

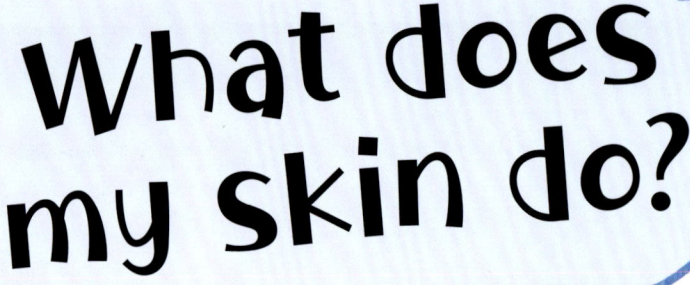

 **Skin protects you from bumps and scratches.** It stops your body from drying out, and prevents germs from getting in. When you play on bikes or skateboards, you should wear gloves and knee pads to protect your skin.

Gloves protect from scrapes.

Knee pads protect from cuts.

Ouch! Ouch! Ouch!

There are millions of tiny touch sensors in your skin. They tell your brain when something touches your skin. Some sensors feel hot and cold. Others feel pain. Ouch!

How thick is my skin?

Your skin is very thin. It is less than 0.1 inches thick. On top is a layer of tough, dead cells called the epidermis. These cells gradually rub off. New cells grow underneath to replace them. Underneath is another layer of skin called the dermis. This contains areas that give you your sense of touch.

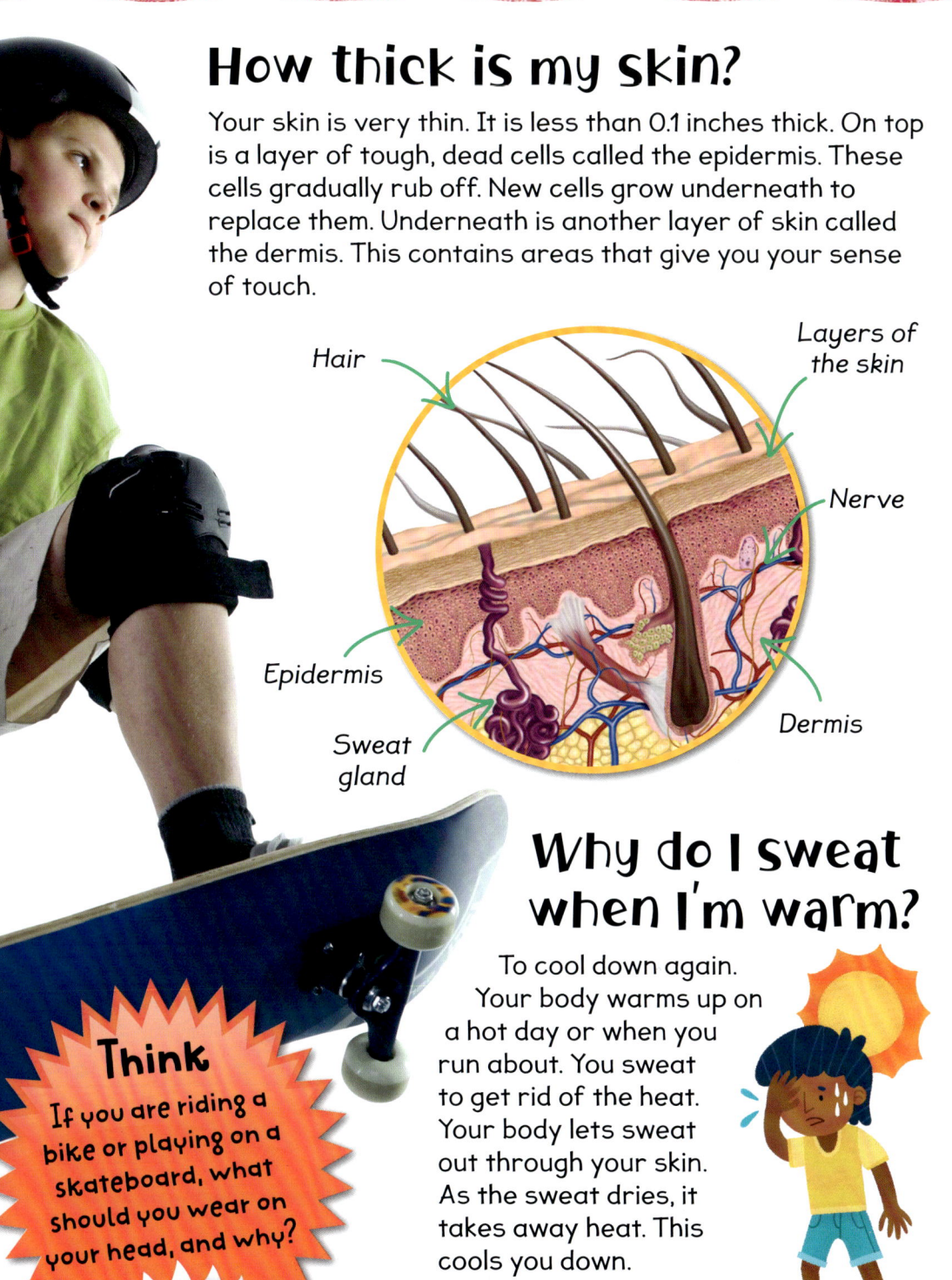

Layers of the skin — Hair, Nerve, Dermis, Epidermis, Sweat gland

Why do I sweat when I'm warm?

To cool down again. Your body warms up on a hot day or when you run about. You sweat to get rid of the heat. Your body lets sweat out through your skin. As the sweat dries, it takes away heat. This cools you down.

Think

If you are riding a bike or playing on a skateboard, what should you wear on your head, and why?

How many bones do I have?

Most people have 206 bones. Half of them are in your hands and feet. All your bones together make up your skeleton. The skeleton is like a frame. It holds up the other parts of your body. It also protects the squashy bits inside.

Human skeleton

Find
Can you find your collarbone? It starts at your shoulder and runs to the top of your rib cage.

Skeleton key
1. Skull
2. Collarbone
3. Shoulder blade
4. Ribs
5. Upper arm bone
6. Pelvis
7. Thigh bone
8. Kneecap
9. Calf bone
10. Shinbone

Strong bones

Your bone is lightweight but super-strong. It is stronger than concrete or steel, which are used for making buildings and bridges! But bones can still break if they are bent too much.

What are bones made from?

Bones are made from different materials mixed together. Some of the materials are very hard and some are tough and bendy. Together they make bones very strong. There is a kind of jelly called marrow inside some bones. This makes tiny parts for your blood, called red and white cells.

Marrow

Spongy bone

Hard bone

How are bones joined together?

Your bones are connected by joints. They let your back, arms, legs, fingers, and toes move. You have about 100 joints in your body. The largest of your joints are in your hips and knees. The smallest joints are inside your ear.

How do muscles work?

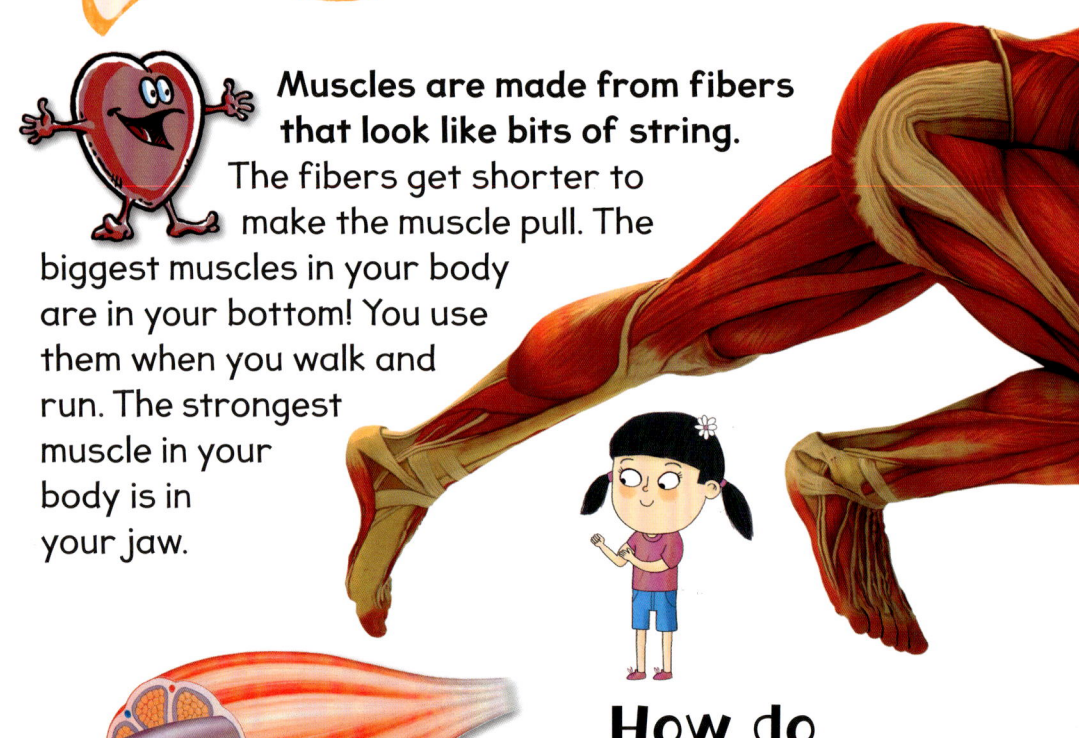

Muscles are made from fibers that look like bits of string. The fibers get shorter to make the muscle pull. The biggest muscles in your body are in your bottom! You use them when you walk and run. The strongest muscle in your body is in your jaw.

Muscle
Muscle fiber
Nerve branches

How do joints bend?

Muscles make your joints, such as your elbows and knees, bend. They help you to run, jump, hold, and lift things. In fact you need muscles to move all of your body.

Cheeky muscles

Your face is full of muscles. You use them to smile, to wrinkle your nose, or to cry. You use more muscles to frown than to smile!

What makes my muscles move?

Your brain does. It sends messages along nerves to your muscles. Lots of muscles are needed for even small movements, like writing with a pen. Your brain controls other muscles without you thinking about it. For example, the muscles in your heart keep working even when you are asleep.

Human skeletal muscles

Feel

Bend and unbend your arm. Can you feel your arm muscles getting shorter and longer?

Why do I need to breathe?

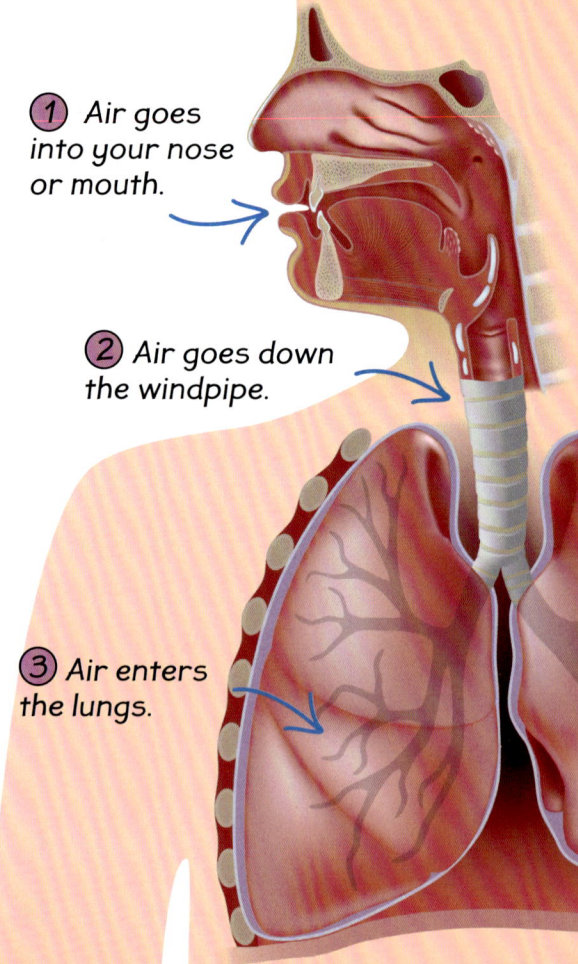

You breathe to take air into your body. There is a gas in the air called oxygen that your body needs to work. The air goes up your nose or into your mouth. Then it goes down a tube called the windpipe and into your lungs.

① Air goes into your nose or mouth.

② Air goes down the windpipe.

③ Air enters the lungs.

Count
How many times do you breathe in and out in one minute?

Is my voice kept in a box?

Not quite! The real name for your voice box is the larynx. It's at the top of the windpipe, and makes a bulge at the front of your neck. Air passing through the voice box makes it shake, or vibrate. This is the sound of your voice. Your voice can make lots of sounds, and helps you to sing!

Children singing

Fill 'em up

When you are resting, you take in enough air to fill a soda can in every breath. When you are running, you breathe in ten times as much air.

What makes air go into my lungs?

There is a big muscle under your lungs that moves down. More muscles make your ribs move out, making your lungs bigger. Air rushes into your lungs to fill the space and when your muscles relax, the air is pushed out again.

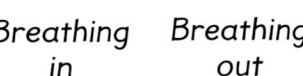

Breathing in   Breathing out

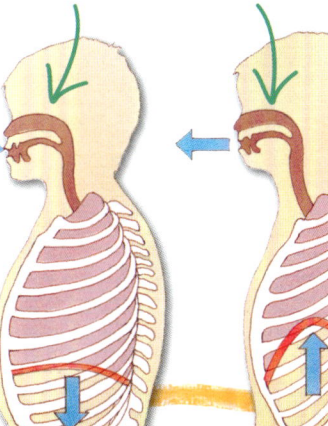

Why does my heart beat?

Blood from body

Blood to lungs

Blood from lungs

To pump blood and oxygen around your body. Your heart is about the size of your fist and is made of muscle. When it beats, your heart squeezes blood into tubes. These tubes carry blood and oxygen around your body. The blood then comes back to the heart from the lungs, with more oxygen.

Blood from body

Beat of life

Your heart beats once a second for the whole of your life. That is 86,000 beats a day, and 31 million beats a year. In total, this is 2 billion beats in your life.

What does blood do?

Your whole body needs oxygen to work. Blood carries oxygen to every part of your body in its red cells. Blood also contains white cells that fight germs and platelets that form a plug to stop you bleeding from a cut.

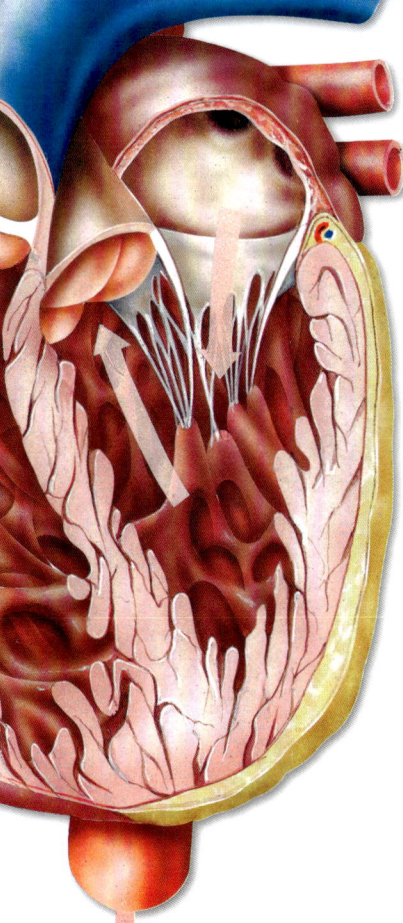

Blood to body

Blood to lungs

Blood from lungs

Feel
Touch your neck under your jaw. Can you feel the blood flowing through an artery to your brain?

Does blood get dirty?

Yes, it does. Because blood carries waste away from your body parts, it has to be cleaned. This is done by your kidneys. They take the waste out of the blood and make a liquid called urine. This liquid leaves your body when you go to the toilet.

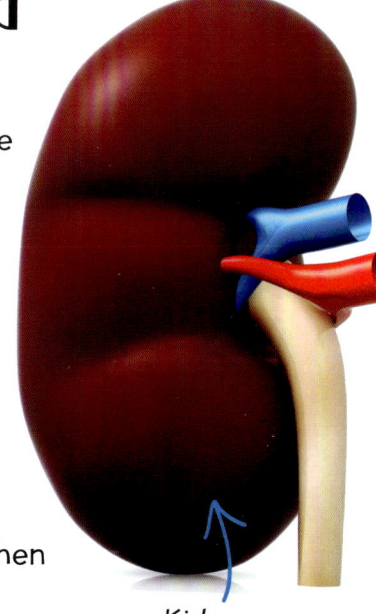

Kidney

Blood to body

Is my brain really big?

Cerebrum

Your brain is about the same size as your two fists put together. It is the place where you think, remember, feel happy or sad—and dream. Your brain also takes information from your senses and controls your body. The main part is called the cerebrum.

Right and left
Your brain has two sides. Each half controls the opposite side of your body. If you throw a ball with your left hand, the right side of your brain told it to!

Cerebellum controls muscles

Brain stem

Can my brain really wave?

Brain waves from an EEG machine.

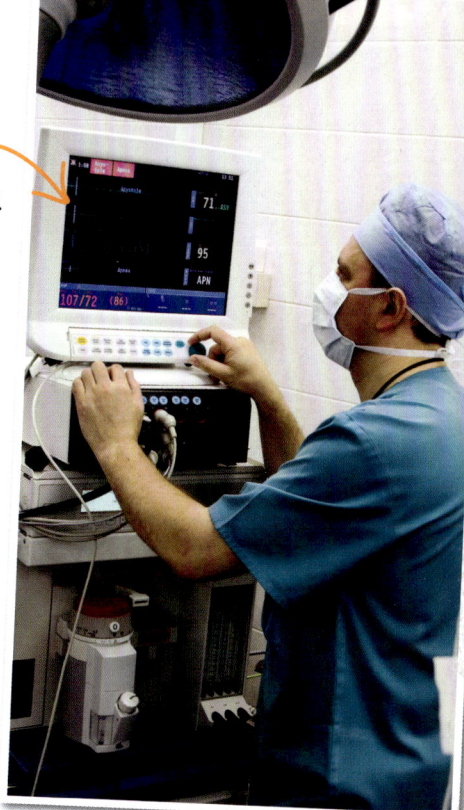

Well, sort of! Your brain works using electricity. It has about 10 billion tiny nerve cells. Tiny bursts of electricity are always jumping around between the cells. Doctors can see your brain working by looking at the electricity with a special machine called an EEG. It shows the electricity as waves on a screen.

Find out
Your brain controls your five senses. Can you find out what they are?

How does my brain help me to play?

Different parts of your brain do different jobs. One part senses touch. Another part deals with thinking. Speaking is controlled by a different part. The cerebellum controls all your muscles. When you play and run, the cerebellum sends messages to your muscles to make them move.

Where did Earth come from?

Earth came from a cloud of dust. The dust whizzed around the Sun at top speed and began to stick together to form lumps of rock. The rocks crashed into each other to make planets, and one of them was Earth.

A cloud of dust spun around the Sun.

Lumps of rock began to form.

Why does the Moon look lumpy?

Big rocks from space, called meteorites, have crashed into the Moon and made dents on its surface. These dents are called craters and they give the Moon a lumpy appearance.

Look

At night, use some binoculars to look at the Moon. Can you see craters on its surface?

The Earth was formed from the lumps of rock.

What is Earth made of?

Earth is a huge ball-shaped lump of rock. Most of Earth's surface is covered by water—this makes the seas and oceans. Rock that is not covered by water makes the land.

Face the Moon

The Moon travels around Earth. We only ever see one side of the Moon's surface.

Why does Earth spin?

Morning

Earth is always spinning. This is because it was made from a spinning cloud of gas and dust. As it spins, Earth leans a little to one side. It takes Earth 24 hours to spin around once. This period of time is called a day.

Evening

Spinning Earth

Discover
There are 24 hours in a day. How many minutes are there in one hour?

Hot and cold

In the Caribbean, the sea can be as warm as a bath. In the Arctic, it is so cold that it often freezes over.

Midday

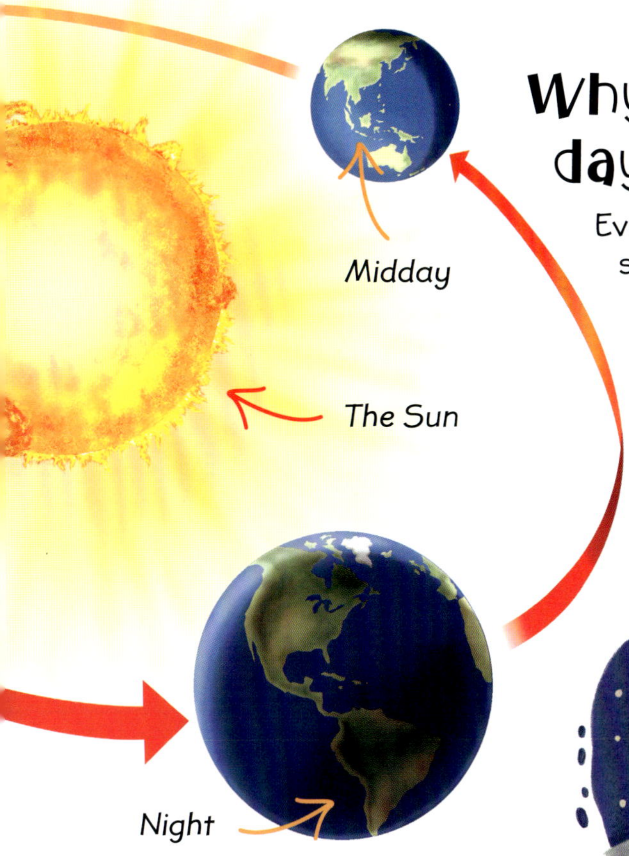

Why do we have day and night?

Every day, each part of Earth spins toward the Sun, and then away from it. When a part of Earth is facing the Sun, it is daytime there. When that part is facing away from Earth, it is nighttime.

The Sun

Night

Do people live on the Moon?

No, they don't. There is no air on the Moon so people cannot live there. Astronauts have visited the Moon in space rockets. They wore special equipment to help them breathe.

What is inside Earth?

Crust

There are different layers inside Earth. There is a thin, rocky crust, a solid area called the mantle, and a center called the core. The outer part of the core is made of hot, liquid metal. The inner core is made of solid metal.

Natural magnet
There is hot, liquid iron near the center of Earth. As Earth spins, the iron acts like a magnet. This is why a compass needle points to North and South.

Active volcano

Find
Use a compass to find North. Does the needle move when you do?

Mantle

Inner core

Outer core

Can we travel into the Earth?

No, we can't. Earth's core is incredibly hot and so far down that no one could ever go there. Sometimes, boiling-hot liquid rock bursts up through Earth's surface from mountains called volcanoes.

Mountains

Does the ground move?

Earth's crust is split into huge areas called plates. Each plate is moving very slowly. If the plates move apart from each other they may cause earthquakes. If they move toward each other they may form volcanoes or mountains.

What is a volcano?

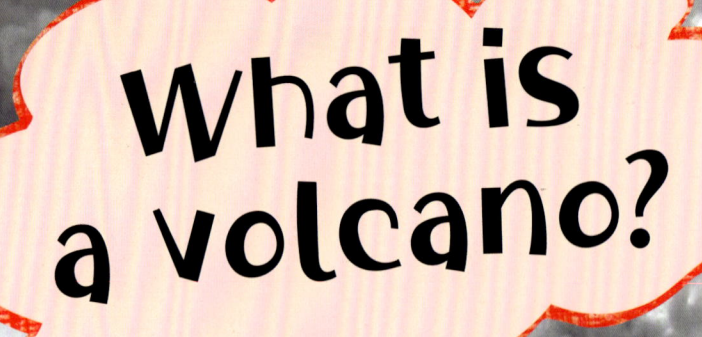

Erupting volcano

A volcano is a mountain that sometimes shoots hot, liquid rock out of its top. Deep inside a volcano is an area called the magma chamber. This is filled with liquid rock. If pressure builds up inside the chamber, the volcano may explode, and liquid rock will shoot out of the top.

Liquid rock

Color
Draw a picture of a volcano erupting. Remember to color the lava bright red.

Magma chamber

How are mountains made?

One way that mountains are formed is when Earth's plates crash together. The crust at the edge of the plates slowly crumples and folds. Over millions of years this pushes up mountains. The Himalayan Mountains in Asia were made this way.

Mountain has been pushed up

What is a range?

A range is the name for a group of mountains. The biggest ranges are the Alps in Europe, the Andes in South America, the Rockies in North America, and the highest of all—the Himalayas in Asia.

The Andes

Layer on layer

When a volcano erupts, the hot lava cools and forms a rocky layer. With each new eruption, another layer is added and the volcano gets bigger.

Why are there earthquakes?

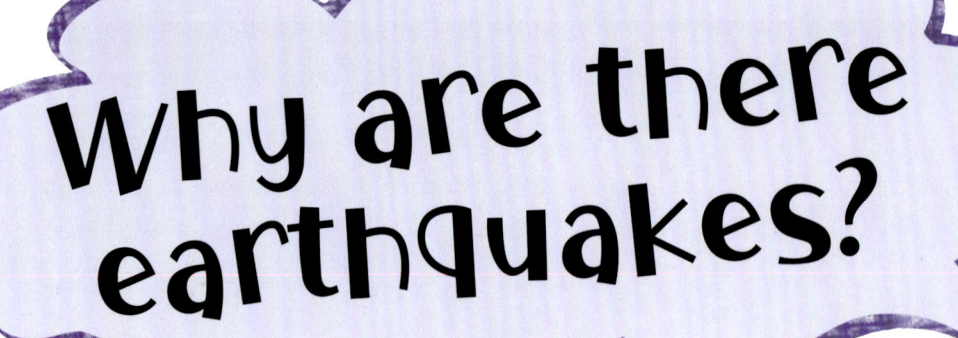

Earthquakes happen when the plates in Earth's crust move apart suddenly, or rub together. They start deep underground in an area called the focus. Land above the focus is shaken violently. The worst part of the earthquake happens above the focus, in an area called the epicenter.

Epicenter

Focus

Remember
Can you remember what it is that breaks at level 5 on the Richter Scale?

38

What is the Richter Scale?

The Richter Scale measures the strength of an earthquake. It starts at level 1 and goes up to level 8. The higher the number, the more powerful and destructive the earthquake.

Super senses
Some people believe that animals can sense when an earthquake is about to happen!

Windows break at level 5.

Bridges and buildings collapse at level 7.

Widespread destruction at level 8.

Can earthquakes start fires?

Yes, a powerful earthquake can cause fires. In 1906, a huge earthquake in San Francisco, California, caused lots of fires. The fires burned down most of the city and the people who lived there became homeless.

Where does rain come from?

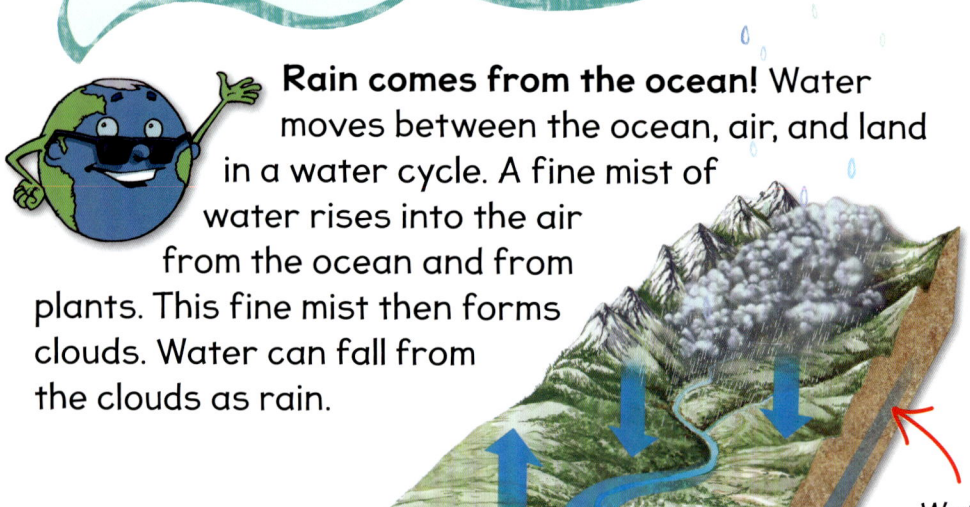

Rain comes from the ocean! Water moves between the ocean, air, and land in a water cycle. A fine mist of water rises into the air from the ocean and from plants. This fine mist then forms clouds. Water can fall from the clouds as rain.

Water vapor rising from the ocean.

Water falling as rain.

Water vapor rising from plants.

Rain flows into rivers.

Head in the clouds!

The tops of tall mountains are often in the clouds. At the top it looks misty. Mountaineers sometimes get lost in these clouds!

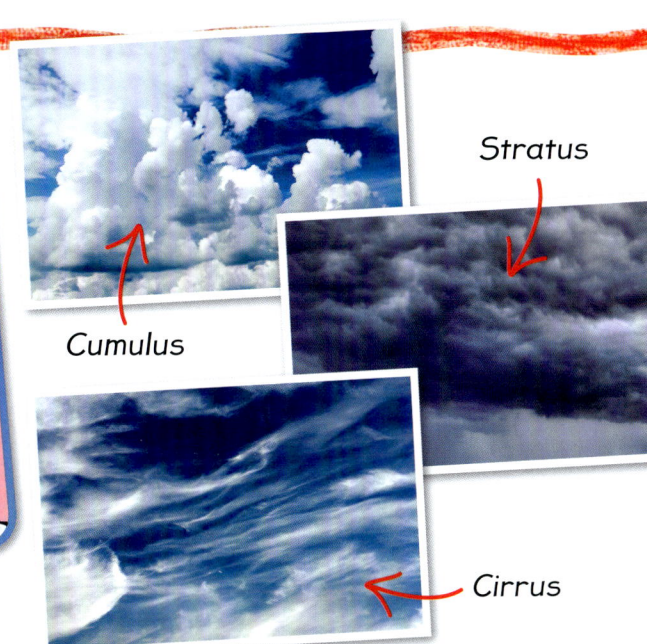

Cumulus

Stratus

Cirrus

Are all clouds small and fluffy?

Clouds come in lots of different shapes and sizes. Weather experts give the different clouds names. Fluffy clouds are called cumulus clouds. Some are small and some are giant. Flat clouds are called stratus clouds. Wispy clouds high in the sky are called cirrus clouds.

What rain never lands?

Sometimes rain that falls from a cloud never reaches the ground. If the drops of rain fall into very dry air, the water turns into gas. This means that the drops disappear and never reach the ground.

Look

Look at the clouds outside. Are they fluffy or flat? The pictures above will help you.

What is snow made of?

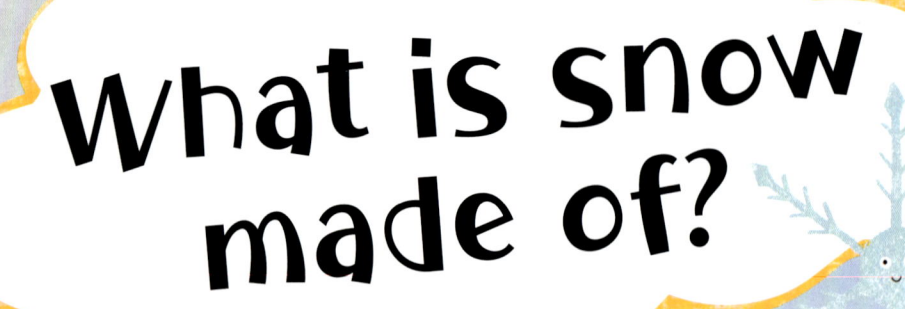

Snow is made of ice, which is water that has frozen. When it is very cold in a cloud, tiny bits of ice (crystals) begin to form, instead of water drops. The pieces clump together to make snowflakes that fall to the ground. The weather must be very cold for snow to fall. If it is too warm, the snowflakes melt and turn to rain.

Shiver!

Antarctica is the coldest place on Earth. The lowest temperature ever recorded there is -129°F. That's much, much colder than inside a freezer!

Avalanche

When is snow dangerous?

When lots of snow falls on mountains, deep layers build up on the slopes. The snow may suddenly slide down the mountain. This is an avalanche. A big avalanche can bury a town. A loud noise or even a person walking on the snow can start an avalanche.

Is snow really white?

Snow is actually made up of millions of individual snow crystals that are clear and colorless, not white. Each of these crystals has lots of tiny surfaces that reflect white light, so when you get big piles of them all together—as snow— it looks white.

Think
Can you think why it could be dangerous to ski across a steep hillside covered with snow?

Is there only one big ocean?

Earth is covered by one giant ocean. We split this into five oceans, which all flow into each other—the Arctic, Atlantic, Pacific, Indian, and Southern. The land we live on, the continents, rises out of the oceans. More than two thirds of Earth's surface is covered by oceans—there is more than twice as much ocean as land!

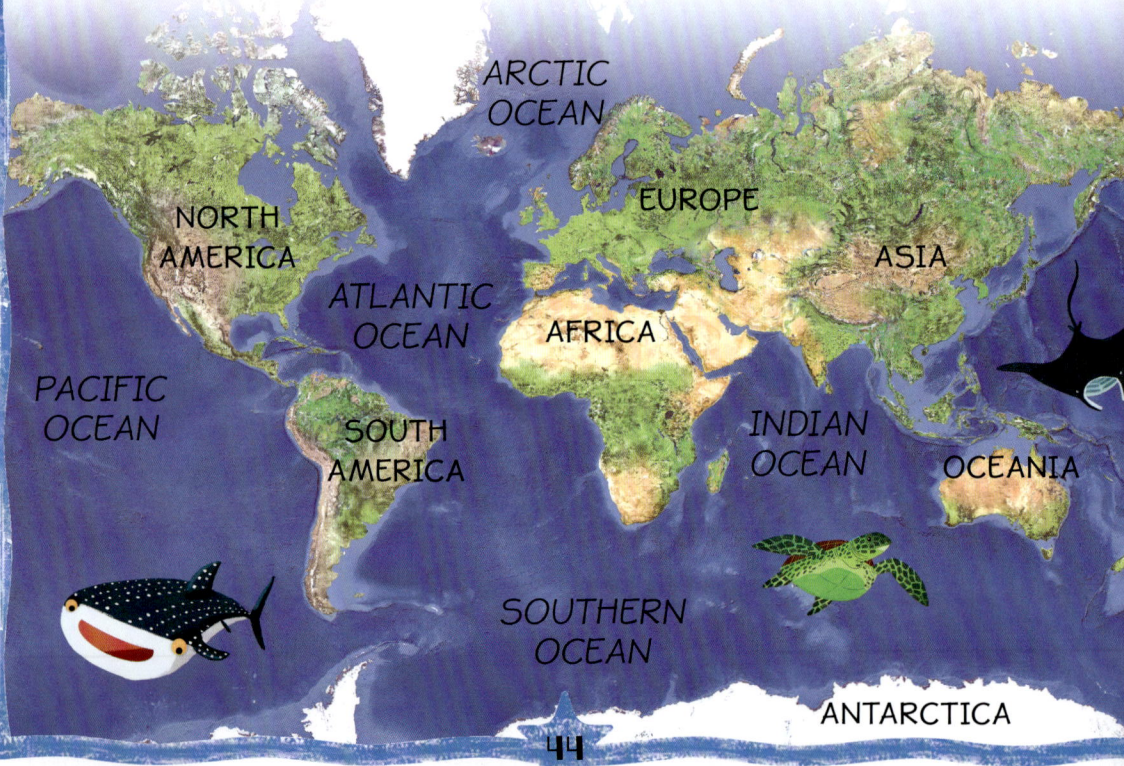

ARCTIC OCEAN

NORTH AMERICA

EUROPE

ASIA

ATLANTIC OCEAN

AFRICA

PACIFIC OCEAN

SOUTH AMERICA

INDIAN OCEAN

OCEANIA

SOUTHERN OCEAN

ANTARCTICA

Are there mountains under the sea?

Yes there are. The land beneath the sea looks a lot like the land above the sea. It is covered by mountains, flat areas called plains, and deep valleys called trenches.

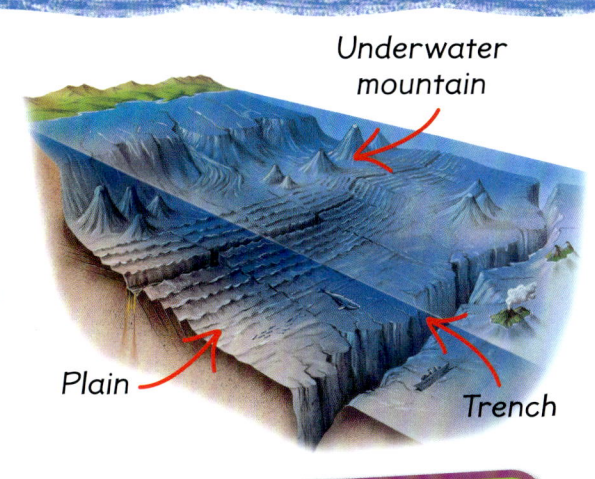

Underwater mountain

Plain

Trench

Salty and fresh
Almost all of the world's water is in the oceans. Only a tiny amount is in freshwater lakes and rivers.

Where do islands come from?

Islands are "born" beneath the sea. If an underwater volcano erupts, it throws out hot, sticky lava. This cools and hardens in the water. Layers of lava build up and up, until a new island peeps above the waves.

Find
Look at the world map to find where you live. Which ocean is nearest to you?

Island

Do seashells have feet?

Tiny animals called limpets live inside some seashells. They stick to rocks at the shoreline where they eat slimy, green plants called algae. When the tide is out, limpets stick to the rocks like glue, with a strong muscular foot. They only move when the tide crashes in.

Limpets

Can starfish grow arms?

Yes they can. Starfish may have as many as 40 arms, called rays. If a hungry crab grabs hold of one, the starfish abandons its arm and uses the others to get away. It then begins to grow a new arm.

Anemone

Starfish

46

Fighting fit

Anemones are a kind of sea-living plant. Some anemones fight over their feeding grounds. Beadlet anemones shoot sharp, tiny hooks at each other until the weakest one gives in.

When is a sponge like an animal?

Sponges are animals! They are simple creatures that filter food from sea water. They can be many different shapes, sizes, and colors.

Sponge

Crab

Sponge

Find

When you next visit a beach, try to find a rock pool. Write a list of what you see.

What is the scariest shark?

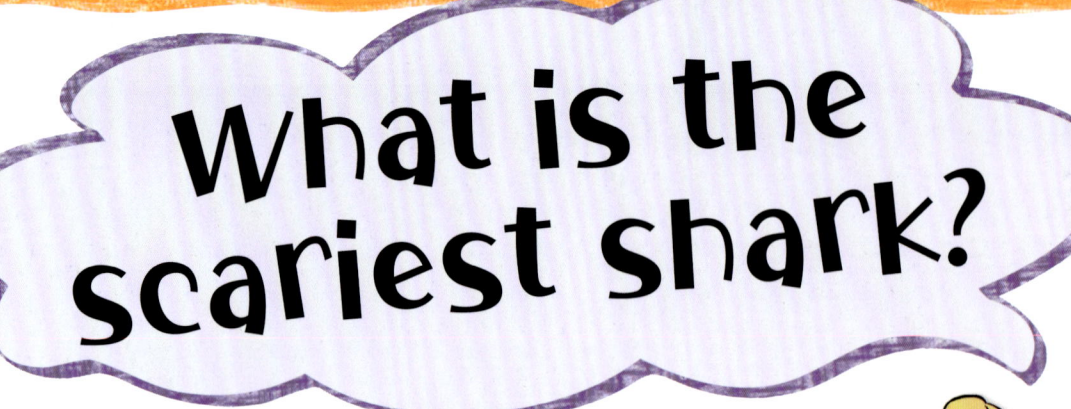

Great whites are the scariest sharks. These huge fish speed through the water at up to 20 miles an hour. Unlike most fish, the great white shark has warm blood. This allows its muscles to work well, but it also means that it needs to eat lots of meat. Great white sharks are fierce hunters. They will attack and eat almost anything, but prefer to feed on seals.

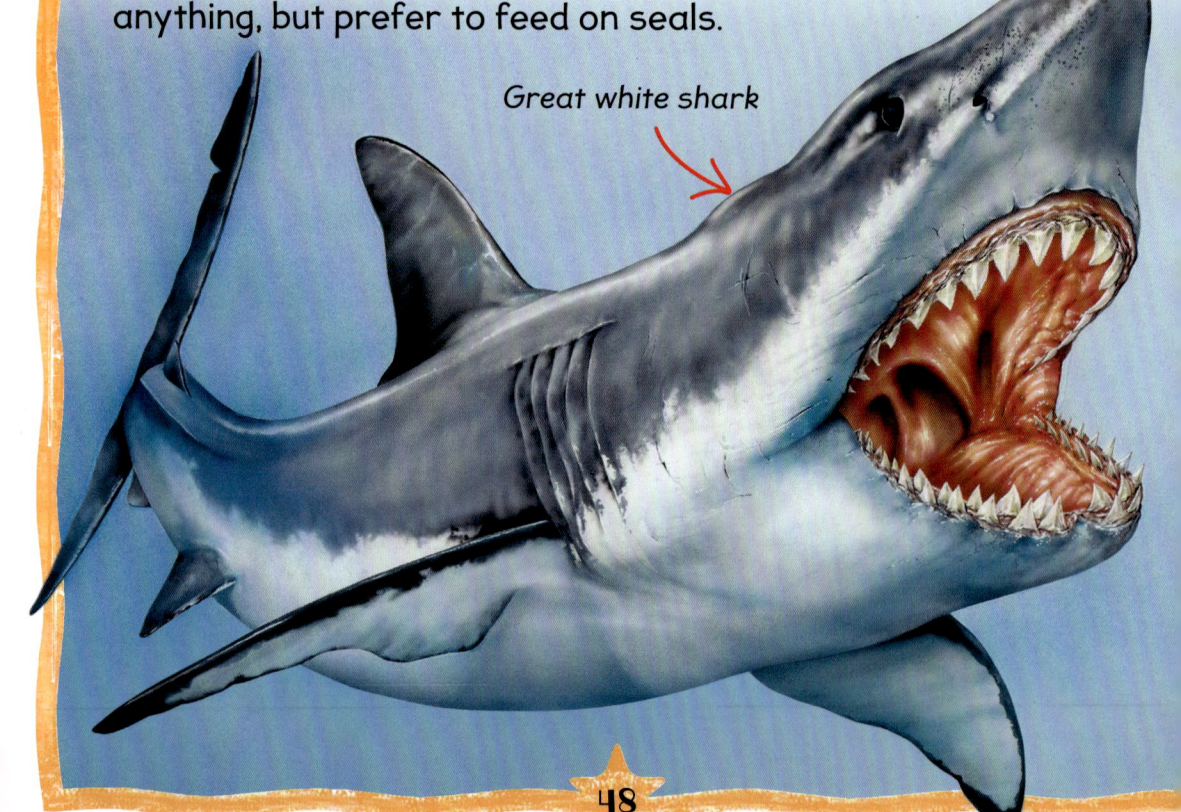

Great white shark

When is a whale not a whale?

Killer whales are also called orcas—but they are actually the biggest member of the dolphin family. Killer whales will kill and eat almost anything in the ocean, from a small fish or seabird to a large whale.

Killer whale attacking a sea lion.

Yum yum!

Most sharks are meat-eaters. Herring are a favorite food for sand tiger and thresher sharks, while a hungry tiger shark will gobble up just about anything!

When is a shark like a pup?

When it's a baby. Young sharks are called pups. Some grow inside their mother's body. Others hatch from eggs straight into the sea.

Draw

Using felt-tip pens, draw your own underwater picture. Include a great white shark.

Who builds walls beneath the sea?

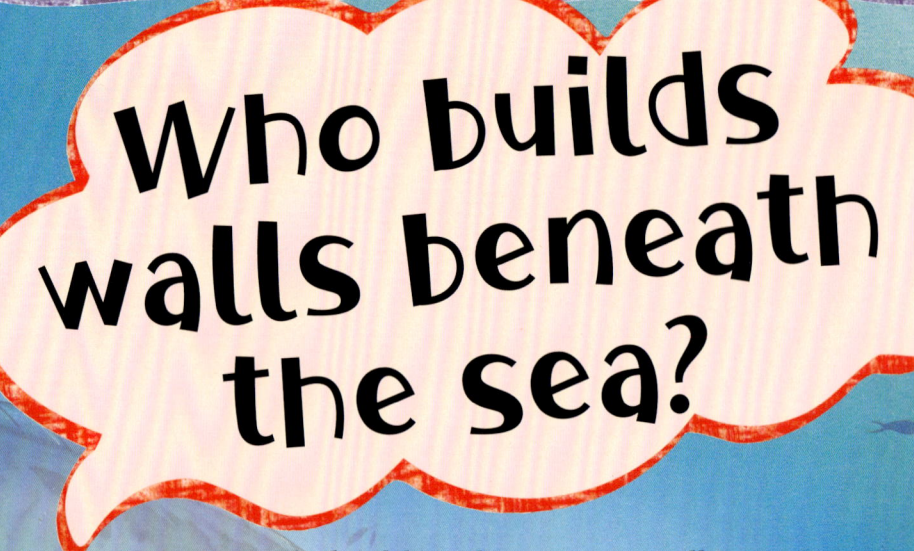

Tiny animals build underwater walls. These walls are made of coral, the leftover skeletons of tiny sea animals called polyps. Over millions of years, enough skeletons pile up to form walls. These make a coral reef. All kinds of creatures live around a reef.

Parrotfish

Seahorse

Clown fish

Look

Do you know where the Great Barrier Reef is? Look in an atlas to find out.

How do fish keep clean?

Cleaner wrasse are little fish that help other fish to keep clean! Larger fish, such as groupers and moray eels, visit the cleaner wrasse, which nibble all the bugs and bits of dirt off the bigger fishes' bodies—what a feast!

Super reef

You can see the Great Barrier Reef from space! At over 1,400 miles long, it is the largest thing ever built by living creatures.

Lionfish

Coral reef

Cleaner wrasse fish

When is a fish like a clown?

When it's a clown fish. These fish are brightly colored. They live among the stinging arms (tentacles) of the sea anemone, where they are safe from predators.

Sea anemone

Can whales sing songs?

All whales make sounds, such as squeaks and moans. The male humpback whale seems to sing, probably to attract a mate. He may repeat his song for up to 20 hours!

Stick around!
Barnacles are shellfish. They attach themselves to ships, or the bodies of gray whales and other large sea animals.

Measure
The blue whale can be 100 feet long. Can you measure how long you are?

Why are whales so big?

Whales have grown to such a huge size because they live in water. The water helps to support their enormous bulk. The blue whale is the biggest animal on the planet. It can weigh up to 165 tons. Every day, it eats about 4 tons of tiny, shrimplike creatures called krill.

Humpback whales

Do whales grow tusks?

The narwhal has a tusk like a unicorn's. This tusk is a long, twirly tooth that comes out of the whale's head. The males use their tusks as weapons when they fight over females. The tusk can grow to 10 feet in length.

Do lions live in the sea?

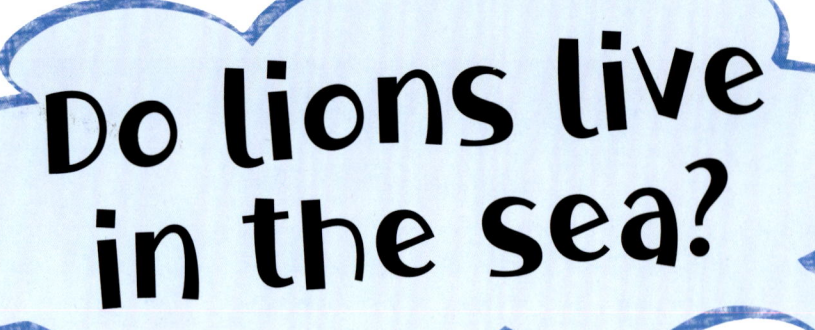

There are lions in the sea, but not the furry, roaring kind. Sea lions, seals, and walruses are all warm-blooded animals that have adapted to ocean life. They have flippers instead of legs—far more useful for swimming. A thick layer of fat under the skin keeps them warm in cold water.

Think
What do you think whales, dolphins, and seals have in common with humans?

Seals

Who can crack open shellfish?

Sea otters can! They balance a rock on their tummy while floating on their back, and crack the shellfish open by banging it on the rock.

Sea otter

Singing seal!

Leopard seals sing in their sleep! These seals, found in the Antarctic, chirp and whistle while they snooze.

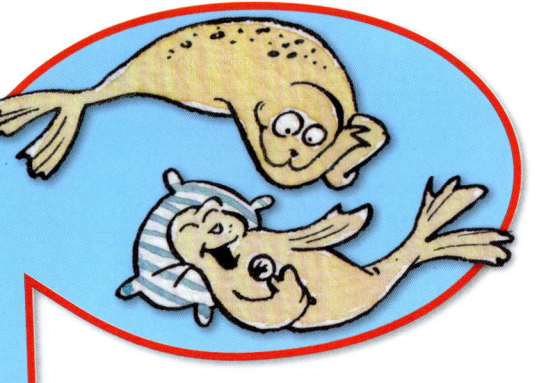

Can a walrus change color?

Walruses seem to change color. In cold water, a walrus can look pale brown or even white. This is because blood drains from the skin to stop the body losing heat. On land, blood returns to the skin and the walrus looks pink!

Are there crocodiles in the sea?

Most crocodiles live in rivers and swamps. The saltwater crocodile also swims out to sea—it doesn't seem to mind the salty water. These crocodiles are huge, and can grow to 23 feet in length and one ton in weight.

Saltwater crocodile

Find
Turtles only come ashore for one reason. Can you do some research and find out why?

Marine iguana

Which lizard loves to swim?

Most lizards live on land, where it is easier to warm up their cold-blooded bodies. Marine iguanas depend on the sea for food and dive underwater to eat seaweed. When they are not diving, they sit on rocks to soak up the sunshine.

Leatherback turtle

How deep can a turtle dive?

Leatherback turtles can dive up to 4,000 feet for their dinner. They are the biggest sea turtles and they make the deepest dives. Leatherbacks feed mostly on jellyfish but also eat crabs, lobsters, and starfish.

Slithery snakes

There are poisonous snakes in the sea. The banded sea snake and the yellow-bellied sea snake both use poison to kill their prey. Their poison is far stronger than that of land snakes.

How do polar bears learn to swim?

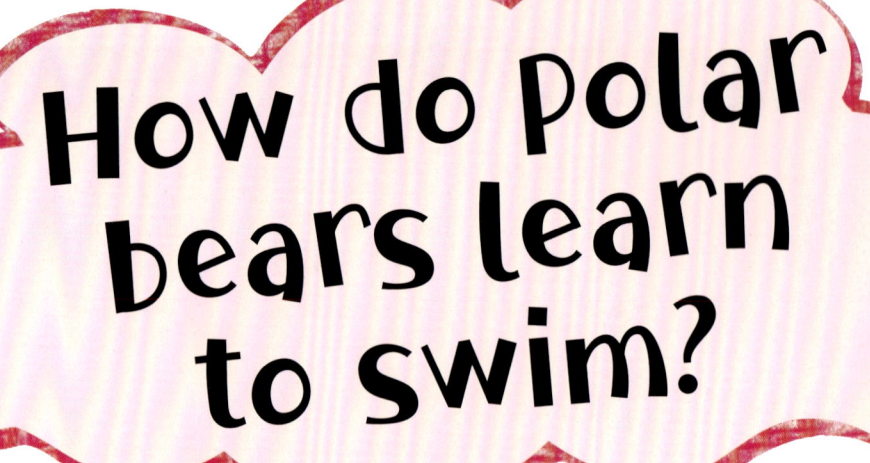

Polar bears live around the freezing Arctic Ocean and are good swimmers. They learn to swim when they are cubs, by following their mother into the water. With their big front paws, the bears paddle through the water. They can swim for many hours.

Polar bear

Imagine
Pretend to be a polar bear. Imagine what life is like at the North Pole.

Are penguins fast swimmers?

Penguins are birds—but they cannot fly. All penguins are fast swimmers. The fastest swimmer is the gentoo penguin. It can reach speeds of 17 miles an hour underwater.

Gentoo penguin

Small and tall!
The smallest penguin is the fairy penguin at just 16 inches tall. The biggest is the emperor penguin at 4 feet in height—as tall as a seven-year-old child!

Which penguin dad likes to babysit?

Emperor penguin dads look after the chicks. The female lays an egg and leaves her mate to keep it warm. The male balances the egg on his feet to keep it off the ice. He goes without food until the chick hatches. When it does, the mother returns and both parents care for it.

How long is the seashore?

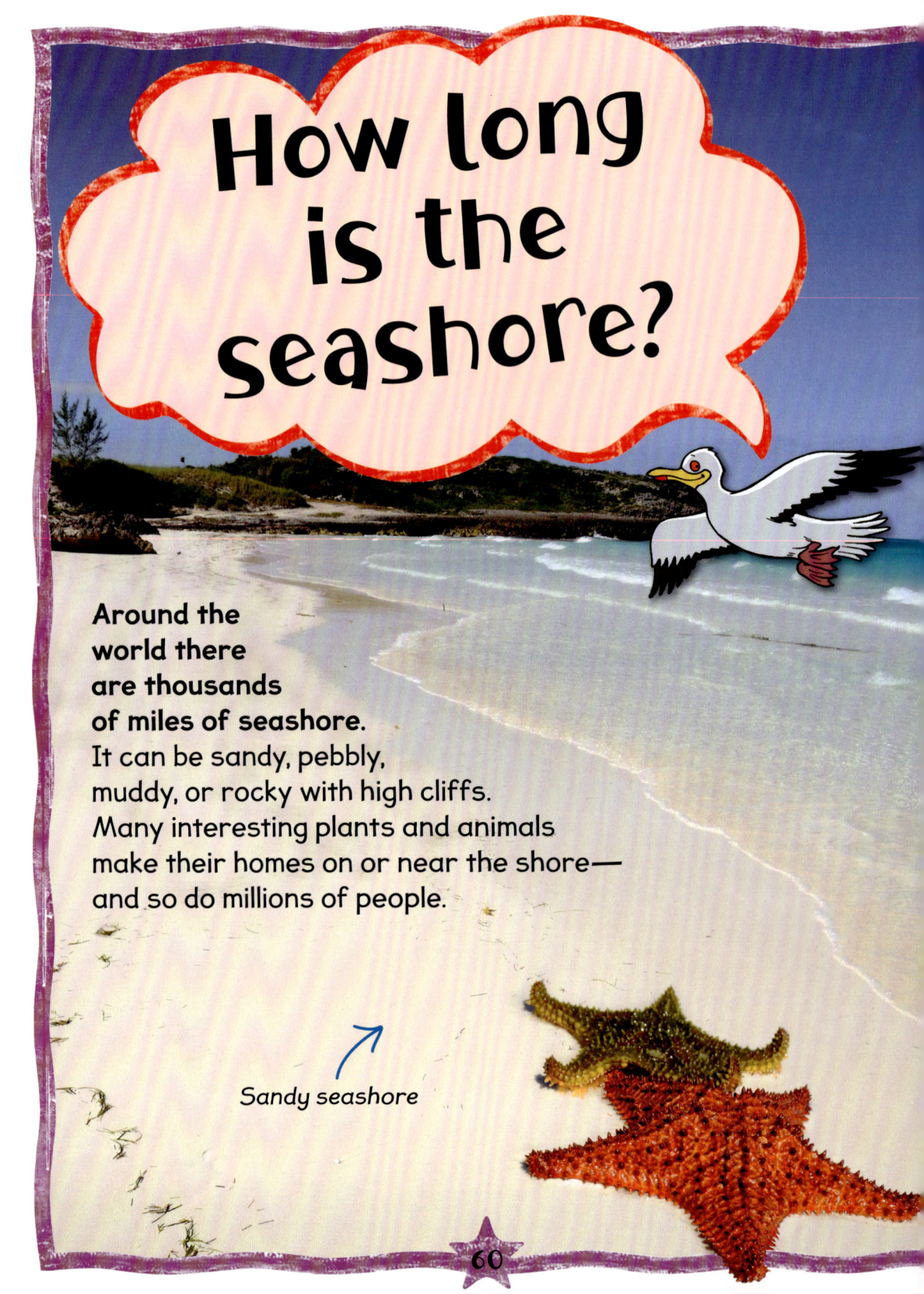

Around the world there are thousands of miles of seashore. It can be sandy, pebbly, muddy, or rocky with high cliffs. Many interesting plants and animals make their homes on or near the shore—and so do millions of people.

Sandy seashore

Which shores are the coldest?

The coldest seashores are around the North and South Poles—the chilliest ends of the Earth. It is so cold that the sea often freezes. Polar bears, penguins, and seals are good at surviving on these icy seashores.

Crabeater seal

Find out
Do you live by the sea? If not, look on a map to find your nearest seashore.

Trees in the breeze
Seashores can be blasted by winds from the sea that constantly blow in the same direction. These winds can make trees grow over to one side.

Why do seashores have tides?

Because the Earth is spinning! As Earth spins, the Moon pulls on the sea, and the surface rises. Water flows up the shore, making a high tide. Then it flows out, creating a low tide. Each seashore has two high tides a day.

High tide
Low tide
Earth
Moon

Why do seashells cling to rocks?

They cling to rocks so they don't get washed away by the tide. Animals such as limpets, mussels, and barnacles live inside seashells. At high tide they open their shells to find food. At low tide, the shells shut tight so they don't dry out.

Limpet

Barnacles

Mussels

Write
When you next visit a sandy beach, try writing your name in the sand with a stick.

What are seashore zones?

The area between high and low tide is called the intertidal zone. Low tide zone is wettest, and has lots of seaweed. High tide zone is drier, and has more land plants.

Fun at the beach
Sandy beaches make a great place for sports, such as kite-flying, soccer, and volleyball.

How big are the biggest waves?

Winds make waves, which break onto the seashore. Some waves can be 100 feet high—taller than a tower of 18 people. The biggest waves are tsunamis, caused by earthquakes shaking the sea.

Why do birds love the seashore?

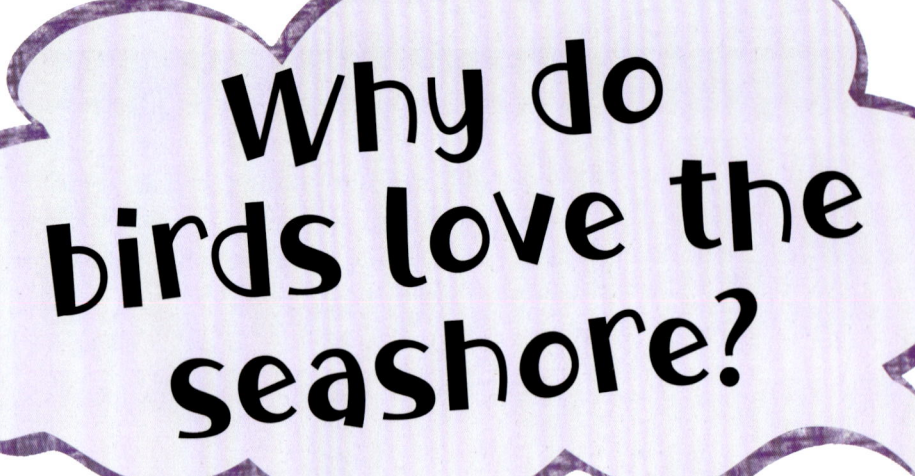

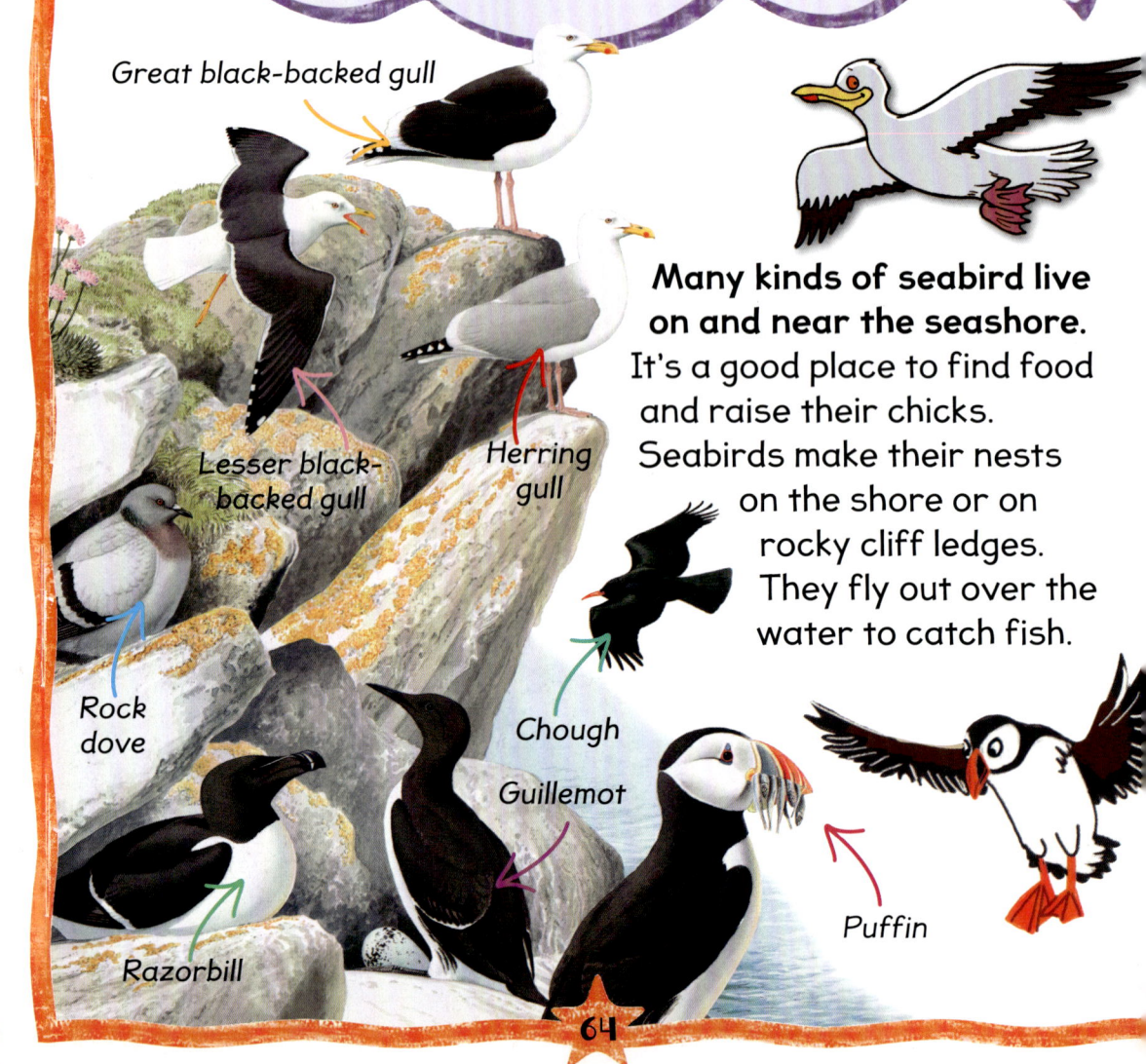

Great black-backed gull

Lesser black-backed gull

Herring gull

Rock dove

Chough

Guillemot

Razorbill

Puffin

Many kinds of seabird live on and near the seashore. It's a good place to find food and raise their chicks. Seabirds make their nests on the shore or on rocky cliff ledges. They fly out over the water to catch fish.

Tiger beetle

Do beetles head for the beach?

The tiger beetle does! This shiny, green beetle lays its eggs in warm, sandy places. These beetles are often found in sand dunes, which are small, grassy hills of sand at the top of a beach.

Paint
Copy the picture on this page and paint a tiger beetle. Add green glitter for its shiny body.

Swimming cats
Some tigers live in mangrove forests near the coast. They like to splash in the water to cool down.

How does being sick help a chick?

Fulmars are seabirds. When they go fishing, they leave their chicks alone in their nests. If hunting animals come near the nests, the chicks squirt stinky, fishy, oily vomit to scare them away!

Does the seashore have shapes?

Sea stack   Arch

Shingle spit

Shingle beach

Yes, seashores have lots of shapes. There are bays, spits, cliffs, archways, and towers. They form over many years, as wind and waves batter the coast. Softer rocks get carved away into bays and hollows. Harder rocks last longer and form sticking-out headlands.

Bay

Make
At a pebbly beach, make a sculpture by balancing small pebbles on top of each other.

Why are pebbles round?

The pebbles on beaches are stones that have been rolled and tumbled around by waves. As they knock together, they lose their sharp corners and edges, and slowly become smooth and round.

Cave

Cliffs

What is sand made of?

Sand is made of tiny pieces of rocks and shells. Larger lumps gradually break down into grains, as the waves crash onto them and make them swirl around.

Delta

Plastic sand

On some beaches, one in every ten sand grains is actually made of plastic. It comes from trash dropped on beaches or thrown from boats.

Sandy beach

What hides in the sand?

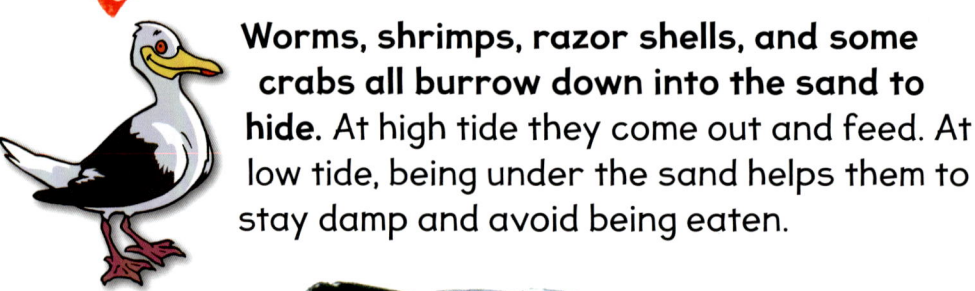

Worms, shrimps, razor shells, and some crabs all burrow down into the sand to hide. At high tide they come out and feed. At low tide, being under the sand helps them to stay damp and avoid being eaten.

Gull

Shrimps

Lugworms

Razor shell

Hunt
Go on a beach treasure hunt. Look for different shells, different-colored pebbles, and seaweed.

Where is the highest tide in the world?

At the Bay of Fundy in Canada, high tide is super-high! The sea level rises to around 56 feet higher than at low tide. At most beaches, the water is just 7–10 feet deeper at high tide.

Treasure-hunting

People love beachcombing too. It's fun to look for interesting creatures, pebbles, shells, or bits of glass that have been rubbed smooth by the sea.

Otter

Lizard

Toad

Crab

Which animals go beachcombing?

A line of seaweed, driftwood, shells, and trash usually collects at the "strandline"— the level the high tide flows up to. Seabirds and other animals, such as foxes and otters, go "beachcombing" along the strandline to look for washed-up crabs and fish to eat.

What is a lagoon?

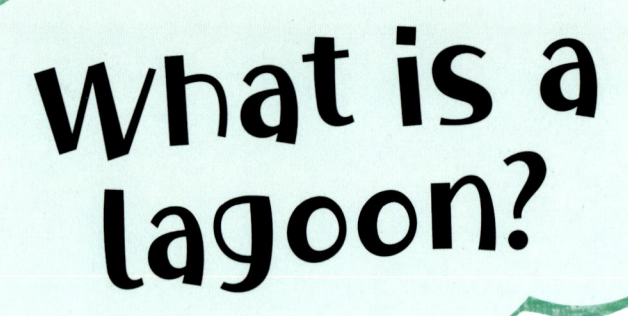

A lagoon is a bit like a shallow lake, but filled with salty seawater. They form when part of the sea is surrounded by a sandbar or a coral reef. Lagoons are warm, shallow and protected from storms— so they make great homes for wildlife.

Lagoon

Make
Build your own sandcastle at the beach or in a sandbox. How tall can you make it?

Which fish can walk on land?

Mudskippers are fish, but they can walk on land! They live in the intertidal zone and can breathe in air or water. They skip over the sand or mud, using their front fins like feet.

Mudskipper

Stingers!
Anemones are seashore creatures with stinging tentacles. They grab and sting prey, then gobble it up!

Why do flamingos have long legs?

Flamingos are tall, pink wading birds. Their long, thin legs help them walk through shallow water in lagoons. They dip their beaks into the water, and use them like a sieve to catch shrimps.

Which forest grows in the sea?

Mangroves are trees that grow in salty water or seaside mud. Some seashores, especially in hot, tropical places, have mangrove forests growing along them. The mangroves' roots stick out of the ground and get covered by the tide when it comes in.

Mangroves

Why do crabs turn the ground bright red?

When red crabs march, they turn the ground into a red, moving mass! These crabs live on Christmas Island in the Indian Ocean. Twice a year, thousands of red crabs head to the sea to lay eggs. Then they go back to their forest homes.

Red crabs

Play
Have a crab race with your friends. You're only allowed to run sideways, like a crab!

Fishy cat
In Southeast Asia there is a wild cat that goes fishing. The fishing cat is a good swimmer, and hunts for fish and other small animals in mangrove swamps.

What is a sea cow?

Sea cows aren't really cows. They are dugongs and manatees—huge sea creatures a bit like seals. Like real cows, sea cows graze on plants, such as sea grass and mangrove leaves.

Dugong

Where do turtles lay their eggs?

Sea turtles live in the sea, but lay their eggs on land. Female turtles crawl up sandy beaches at night, and dig holes with their flippers, in which they lay their eggs. Then they cover them over with sand and leave them to hatch.

Green turtle

Why do baby turtles race to the sea?

When turtle eggs hatch, baby turtles climb out of their sandy nest and head for the sea. They must reach the water quickly, before they get gobbled up by a seabird, crab, or fox.

Salty nose
The marine iguana is a lizard that swims in the sea. As it rests on rocks to warm up, salt from the sea makes a white patch on its nose.

Find out
There are different types of turtle. Look in books or on the Internet to find out what they are.

Puffin

Which seabird has a colorful beak?

Puffins have bright beaks striped with orange, yellow, and black. In spring, their beaks and feet become brighter, to help them find a mate. Males and females rub their beaks together to show they like each other.

What is a plant?

A plant is a living thing that breathes, grows, and changes. Plants live all over the world, even in deserts, on mountains, and underwater. Most plants have flowers, leaves, stems, and roots.

Bud

Flower

Leaf

Stem

Roots

Do bananas grow on trees?

No, but bananas do grow on plants that are almost as tall as trees. A banana plant has one main stem and one big flower. A single bunch of bananas grows from the flower.

Bananas

Potato bug

Big animals eat plants, but so do little ones! Bugs, slugs, and mini-beasts all enjoy nibbling fruits, shoots, roots, and leaves.

Make

Ask a grown-up to help you make a milkshake. You need ice cream, bananas, and milk.

Did dinosaurs eat plants?

Some dinosaurs feasted on meat, but the biggest ones munched on plants. They probably spent all day eating to get enough energy for their giant bodies to keep moving!

Why do flowers like bees?

Bee collecting pollen.

Flowers like bees, and bees like flowers! Bees help flowers to grow seeds and flowers give bees food. Look at a flower and you will see a yellow dust, called pollen. Bees eat pollen and collect it to take back to their hives.

Seedlings

Can plants move?

Plants don't have arms, legs, or wings, but they can still move. All plants need sunlight, and they can bend their stems so their leaves face the Sun.

Grow
Grow some cress seedlings. Look at how the seedlings bend toward the light as they grow.

Pollen coat
Bats are flying animals that come out at night. They feed on flower nectar and can get covered in pollen!

Who knocks nuts?

Birds called nutcrackers do! Nuts are seeds with hard shells. Nutcrackers open nuts by bashing them against rocks. The hard shells fall away, and the bird can eat the seed inside.

How tall can a tree grow?

The tallest trees in the world are called giant redwoods. Some redwoods are more than 300 feet tall—that's enormous! These trees don't just grow tall, they grow old too. A redwood tree can live for 2,000 years or more.

← Giant redwood tree.

Plant
Plant two bean seeds in different pots. Only water one pot. Which seed grows?

Why do hummingbirds hum?

Tiny hummingbirds beat their wings so fast, they make a humming sound. These birds also hover—when they beat their wings they stay in one place. This means they can drink nectar from a flower without having to land on it.

Sun fun

Plants can only make food during the day, when the Sun shines. At night they rest, just like we do.

Cacti

Can plants live in a desert?

Yes they can. Cacti are plants that live in very dry places, and they have tiny spiny leaves. Plants need water to live, but it doesn't often rain in a desert. When it rains, cacti save water in their fat stems.

Why do flowers smell nice?

Butterfly feeding on nectar.

Flowers smell nice because they want animals to visit them. When a butterfly feeds on a flower's nectar, it picks up pollen on its feet and takes it to another flower. There, the pollen joins with an egg and grows into a seed.

Which plants can pop?

Squirting cucumbers can squirt their seeds over 15 feet away! Their seedpods are full of water and pop when they are ripe, sending their brown seeds far and wide.

Make
Ask a grown-up to make popcorn with you. When the air inside the corn gets hot, it pops!

Hungry bugs
Caterpillars spend all day eating leaves and growing. They are so hungry that one caterpillar can eat every leaf on a plant.

Do toads sit on toadstools?

Toads sometimes sit on toadstools, but they prefer to hide in the damp grass and leaves underneath them. Toadstools and mushrooms are types of fungus. Some fungi are very poisonous.

Toadstools and mushrooms

Why do moths need long tongues?

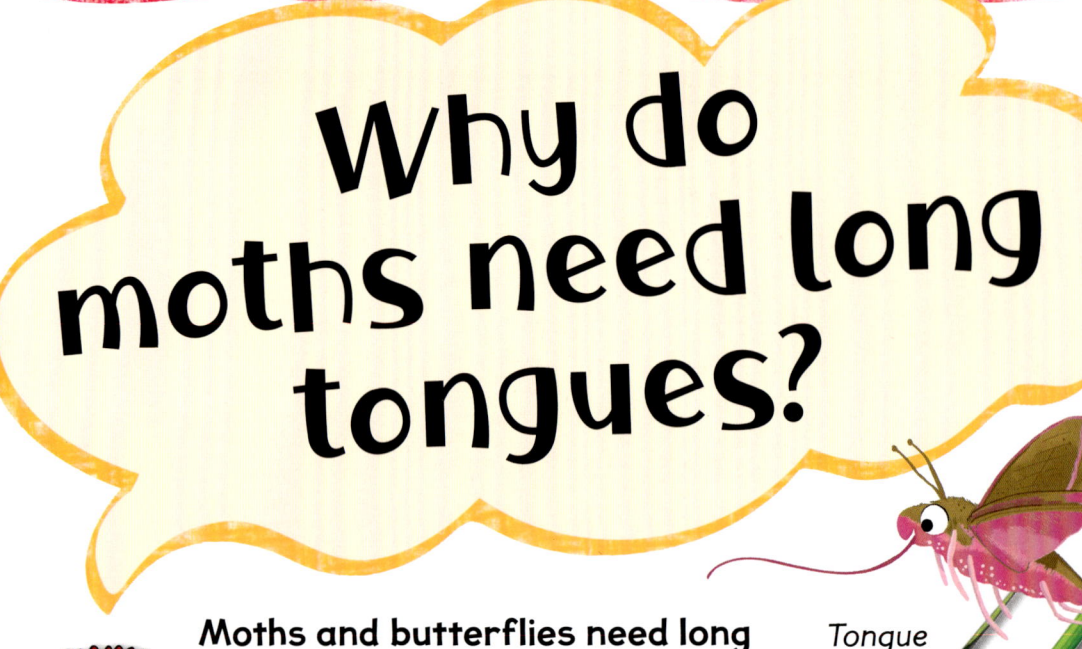

Moths and butterflies need long tongues to reach the nectar deep inside a flower. Nectar is a sugary juice that lots of insects and birds like to drink. It tastes sweet and it gives them lots of energy.

Tongue

Moth feeding on nectar.

What is the biggest flower?

The world's biggest flower is called a rafflesia. One bloom can measure up to 3 feet wide. Rafflesia flowers grow in rain forests. They have a strong, nasty smell to attract insects to them.

Go away!

The spines on a cactus are sharp little leaves. Plants stop animals from eating them with thorns, spines, and even nasty tastes.

Rafflesia flower

Do plants have eyes?

Plants don't have eyes and they cannot see. Sometimes we say that potatoes have "eyes," but these are just the places where roots and stems are starting to grow.

Measure

Use a measuring tape to see how big a rafflesia is. Is it bigger than you?

Why do leaves turn red?

At the end of the summer, leaves begin to die. As they die, their colors turn from green to red, gold, and brown, before they fall from the tree. This time is called fall. During winter, the trees will rest, but they are still alive.

Trees in fall.

How do seeds grow?

When the time is right, seeds begin to grow into new plants. They need water, air, and warmth to grow. First, a small, white root grows. Then, a new green shoot grows up to the light. Soon, new green leaves grow too.

Leaves

Seed

Green shoot

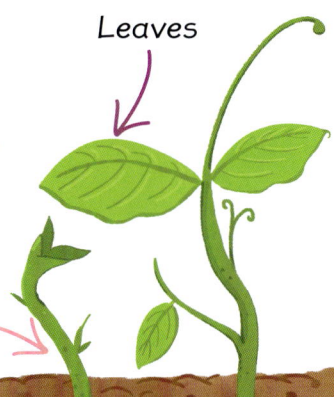

Find
Go on a nature hunt in fall. Ask a grown-up to help you find colorful leaves, berries, conkers, and acorns.

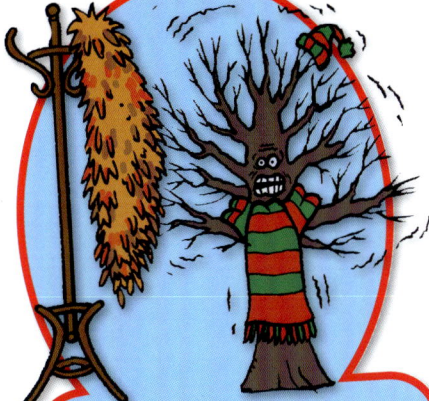

Which tree can you drink from?

In remote places in Australia, indigenous people drink from the paperbark tree if water is scarce. The trunk is full of sweet liquid that is safe to drink.

Brrrrrr!
Trees and plants don't feel the cold like we do, but very frosty weather can kill plants.

Why do plants have teeth?

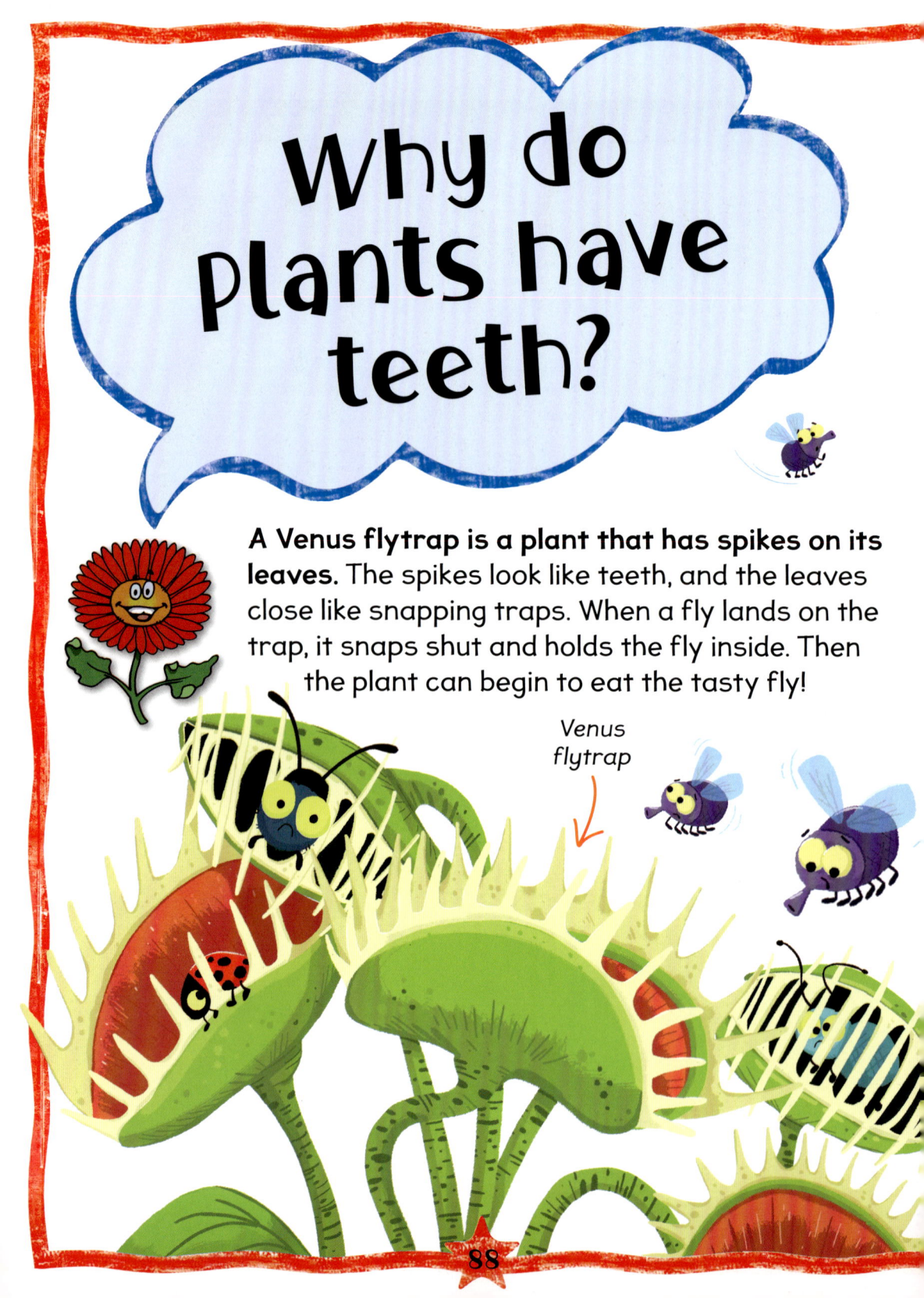

A Venus flytrap is a plant that has spikes on its leaves. The spikes look like teeth, and the leaves close like snapping traps. When a fly lands on the trap, it snaps shut and holds the fly inside. Then the plant can begin to eat the tasty fly!

Venus flytrap

Fussy koalas

Koalas only eat leaves from gum trees. They spend up to 22 hours every day fast asleep, and eat for the rest of the time.

What happens underground?

Plants grow in soil, which is full of tiny animals. Some of these bugs and worms eat roots, but most of them help to make the soil a healthy place for plants to grow.

How do birds help plants?

Birds eat the berries and fruits from plants. When a bird eats a fruit, the seed inside passes through its body and comes out in its poo. This seed may grow into a new plant.

Bird eating berries.

Dig

Ask a grown-up to choose a plant to dig up. Can you find any bugs in the soil around the roots?

Who lives in a rain forest?

Rain forests are home to millions of animals and plants. A place that is home to lots of animals and plants is called a habitat. Rain forests are very special habitats. People live there too.

Draw
What kind of habitat do you live in? Draw a picture of it and color it in.

Which lizard can bark?

There are not many dogs in the jungle, but there are lizards that bark! They are called tokay geckos. Their bark sounds like "to-kay, to-kay." These lizards climb trees and hunt bugs at night.

Macaws

Big mouth
Potoos are jungle birds that eat insects at night. They have big, gaping mouths and swallow their food whole.

Why do parrots talk?

Parrots talk for the same reason we do—they need to tell each other things. When most parrots talk they twitter, screech, and squawk. Some sounds are a warning. They tell other parrots that danger may be nearby.

Why do toucans have big bills?

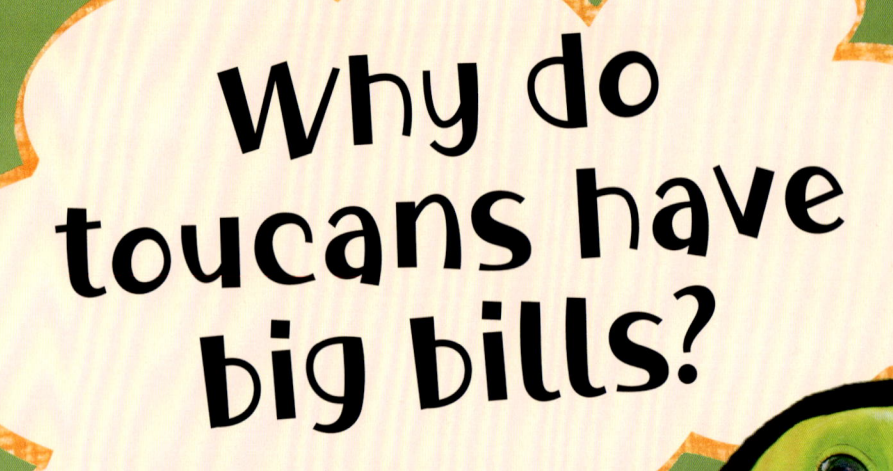

Toucans are birds with big, colorful bills (beaks). Both males and females have big bills, so they might be useful in attracting a mate. They may also help toucans reach and eat fruit high up in the trees.

Toucan

How big is a Goliath spider?

Goliath spiders are huge! They live in the rain forests of South America and can have a leg span of up to 12 inches. They eat insects and sometimes catch small birds to eat. Luckily, these spiders are harmless to people.

Goliath spider

Make
Use a paper plate, pipe cleaners, and tape to make a life-size model of a Goliath spider.

Does it rain every day in a rain forest?

It rains almost every day. This habitat is home to plants that need lots of rain and plenty of hot, sunny days. Without rain and warmth, rain forest plants cannot grow.

Yum yum!
Leeches are sluglike animals that live in rain forest rivers. They love to suck blood from animals and humans!

How slow is a sloth?

Sloths are possibly the slowest animals alive. They are so slow, it is almost impossible to see one moving. Sloths hang upside down in trees. Once a week, they slowly climb to the ground to poo. It takes them one minute to walk 6 feet!

Baby sloth

Does chocolate grow on trees?

No, chocolate doesn't grow on trees, but the beans we use to make chocolate do. They are called cacao beans, and they grow in big pods on cacao trees.

Cacao pods

Scratch and sniff!
Tapirs use their long snouts to sniff for food. They scratch around in mud to find berries and fruit.

Why do monkeys howl?

Monkeys are very noisy animals. They live in groups and need to howl, chatter, and hoot to talk to one another. Howler monkeys live in South American jungles. They are some of the loudest animals in the world.

Go slow
Pretend to be a sloth. Measure 6 feet and see how slowly you can walk that distance.

Which beetle is a giant?

Most beetles are smaller than a fingernail, but one is longer than your hand. It is a Hercules beetle, and males can grow to 7 inches long. They have long horns on their heads, which they use to fight each other.

Hercules beetle

Agouti

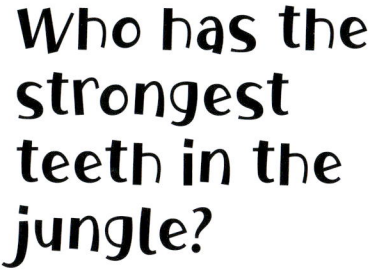

Who has the strongest teeth in the jungle?

Agoutis have such strong teeth they can bite through hard nut shells. Few animals are able to open the tough shells of Brazil nuts. Agoutis can bite through them to eat the tasty nut inside.

Big bird!
A cassowary is a bird, but it cannot fly. Cassowaries have sharp claws on their feet, and they kick out if they're scared by intruders.

Count
If an agouti eats five nuts every day, how many will it eat in two days?

Can a piranha eat a horse?

No, a single piranha can't eat a horse, but a group, or shoal, could. Piranhas are fierce fish that live in some rain forest rivers, and they have very sharp teeth. When a group of piranhas attack, they can eat a big animal in minutes.

What is the biggest butterfly?

Millions of butterflies and moths flutter through the world's rain forests. One of the biggest is Queen Alexandra's bird-wing butterfly. It can measure nearly 11 inches from wing tip to wing tip.

Queen Alexandra's bird-wing butterfly

Why are jungle frogs so deadly?

Not all jungle frogs are deadly, but some have poisonous skin. Most poison arrow frogs are small and have colorful skin that is coated with poison. The golden poison arrow frog is one of the deadliest of all, but it is no bigger than your thumb.

Golden poison arrow frog

Bug cleaner!
Ring-tailed lemurs roll giant millipedes over their fur! It's thought that the millipedes release a chemical that keeps pesky flies and bugs off the lemurs.

Who eats all the leaves?

The floor of the forest is covered with dead leaves. Some of them will rot away. Others will be eaten by the billions of tiny animals that live in a jungle, such as ants, caterpillars, slugs, and snails.

Find
Look under plants and stones to see garden animals, such as ants, beetles, and pill bugs. Try not to disturb them.

Are there dragons in the jungle?

There are no real dragons in the jungle, but there are lizards that look like dragons! Boyd's dragon is an iguana that has a flap of skin under its chin, called a dewlap. It also has a row of spines that run along its back.

Boyd's dragon

When is a leaf not a leaf?

When it is a leaf insect! Some rain forest insects pretend to be leaves or sticks. This means they can stay still and hide from birds and lizards that want to eat them. They can also hide from bugs they want to catch.

Leaf insect

Freeze
Lie on the floor like a leaf insect and stay still for as long as you can.

Yummy honey!
Sun bears have very strong claws for digging into bees nests. They lick out the honey with their long tongues.

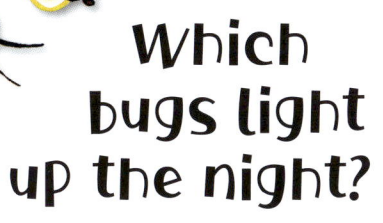

Which bugs light up the night?

Glowing insects do. Some of these bugs are called glow-worms and others are called fireflies. Hundreds of them gather in a tree and twinkle like Christmas lights, or stars in the sky.

Which bird is Lord of the Jungle?

The Philippine eagle is called the "Lord of the Jungle." It is one of the biggest birds in the world. This eagle has huge talons (claws) and a strong, curved bill. It hunts other birds, snakes, wild cats, lemurs, and even monkeys.

Philippine eagle

Flying lemur

When is a toad like a leaf?

When it is hidden on the forest floor! Some jungle frogs and toads have colors and patterns that help them to hide on trees, leaves, or branches. The leaflitter toad has brown camouflage that makes it look like a dead leaf.

Leaflitter toad

Tongue-twister!

Okapis have very long tongues. They are so long, an okapi can use its tongue to lick its eyeballs clean!

Why are some animals rare?

When the number of a species (type) of animal falls, it is said to be rare. Tigers, orangutans, and gorillas are rare. Animals become rare when they cannot find enough food or their home in the wild has gone.

Think
Make up a story about three jungle animals and an adventure they have.

Why does a snake squeeze its food?

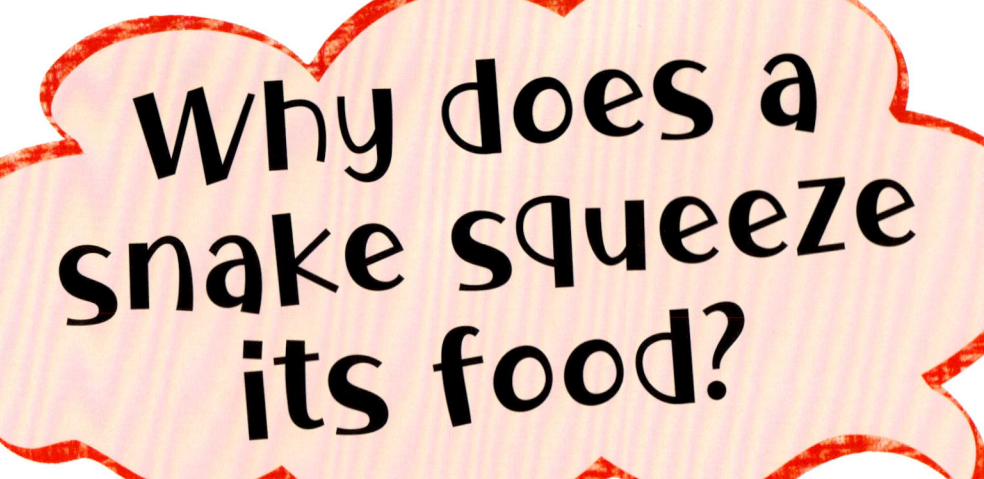

So it can eat it! The emerald tree boa is a rain forest snake. Once it has grabbed its prey, it wraps its body around it and squeezes it to death. This snake can grow to 6 feet long.

Emerald tree boa

Forest elephants

Who has the biggest teeth in the jungle?

Elephants have the biggest teeth, called tusks. African forest elephants have tusks that point down, so they can walk through plants and trees without getting their tusks tangled in leaves!

Record
It rains almost every day in rain forests. Make a chart to record the weather every day for one month.

Do monkeys have beards?

Mangabey monkeys have tufts of white hair that look like beards! These may help the monkeys to communicate. Mangabeys live in Africa, in groups called "troops."

Sticky toes!
Gecko lizards are able to crawl on rocks and trees because they have sticky toes. Tiny hairs on their toes work like glue, to make them stick.

What is the biggest cat?

The Siberian tiger is the biggest cat, and one of the largest meat-eating animals in the world. The heaviest Siberian tiger on record weighed 1,025 pounds—that's the same weight as 23 of you! It has thick fur to help it survive in freezing conditions.

Where do tigers live?

Tigers only live in southern and eastern Asia, in forests, woodlands, and swamps. They used to live in much larger areas, but humans have now built houses and farms on much of the land. Siberian tigers live in snow-covered forests where temperatures can be −58°F.

Siberian tiger

Hair-head!
Male lion cubs begin to grow thick fur around their head and neck, called a mane, when they are about three years old.

Why do lion cubs have to leave home?

Male lion cubs don't get to stay with their family group or pride—they get pushed out at about three years old. By then they are old enough to look after themselves. Soon they will take over new prides and have their own cubs.

Discover
Look on a map and see if you can find the parts of the world where tigers live.

Do big cats live in groups?

Lions are the only big cats that live in large family groups, called prides. A pride is normally made up of four to six female lions, one or two males, and their cubs. Some prides may have up to 30 lions if there is plenty of food nearby.

Which cats can scream?

Small cats such as pumas make an ear-piercing scream instead of a roar. The cat family can be divided into two groups—big cats that can roar and small cats that can't. A screaming cat can still be just as frightening!

Why are lions lazy?

Lions seem lazy, but they have to rest to keep cool in the hot African sun. Usually, lions rest for around 20 hours a day. They normally hunt in the morning or at night when it's coolest. After a big meal they don't need to eat again for several days.

Lady-lion hunt!

Female lions, called lionesses, do nearly all of the hunting for the pride. Male lions will only help with the hunt if it's a big animal, such as a buffalo or giraffe.

Pretend

Imagine you are a prowling lion creeping up on your prey. See how slowly and quietly you can move.

Pride of lions

Are tigers always orange?

Most tigers are orange but a very small number are born white. All tigers have stripes. These help them to blend into their shadowy, leafy surroundings, making hunting easier. White tigers born in the wild are less likely to live as long as orange tigers because they do not blend in as well.

White tiger

Lynx

Which cat is in danger?

Lynx numbers are falling because of the drop in the number of rabbits, which are their main food. The Iberian lynx, found in Spain and Portugal, is the most endangered cat. This is because humans have cut down many forests where they live.

What do ocelots eat?

Ocelots, also called "painted leopards," are small wild cats found mainly in South and Central America. They eat lots of different foods including rats, birds, frogs, monkeys, fish, tortoises, and deer.

Think
How many types of food do you eat in a day? Is it as many as an ocelot?

Going, gone!
It's too late for some big cats. The Taiwan clouded leopard, and the Caspian, Bali, and Javan tigers are extinct (have died out).

Why do leopards climb trees?

Leopards climb trees to rest or to eat their food in safety. These big cats often kill prey that is larger than themselves. They are excellent climbers and are strong enough to drag their prey up into a tree, away from other hungry animals.

Leopard with its prey.

Paint
Using face paints, ask an adult to make your face spotty like a leopard's.

How can humans help big cats?

Humans can help big cats by protecting areas of rain forest and grassland where they live. These areas are called reserves. In a reserve, trees are not allowed to be cut down and the animals can live in safety.

Puma

No boat? Float!
Ancient Chinese soldiers used blown-up animal skins to cross deep rivers. They used their mouths to blow in air, then covered them with grease to keep it in.

What is a puma's favorite food?

Rabbits, hares, and rats are the favorite foods of a puma. They will attack bigger animals too. In places where humans have built their homes near the puma's natural surroundings, people have been attacked by these cats.

Where do cheetahs live?

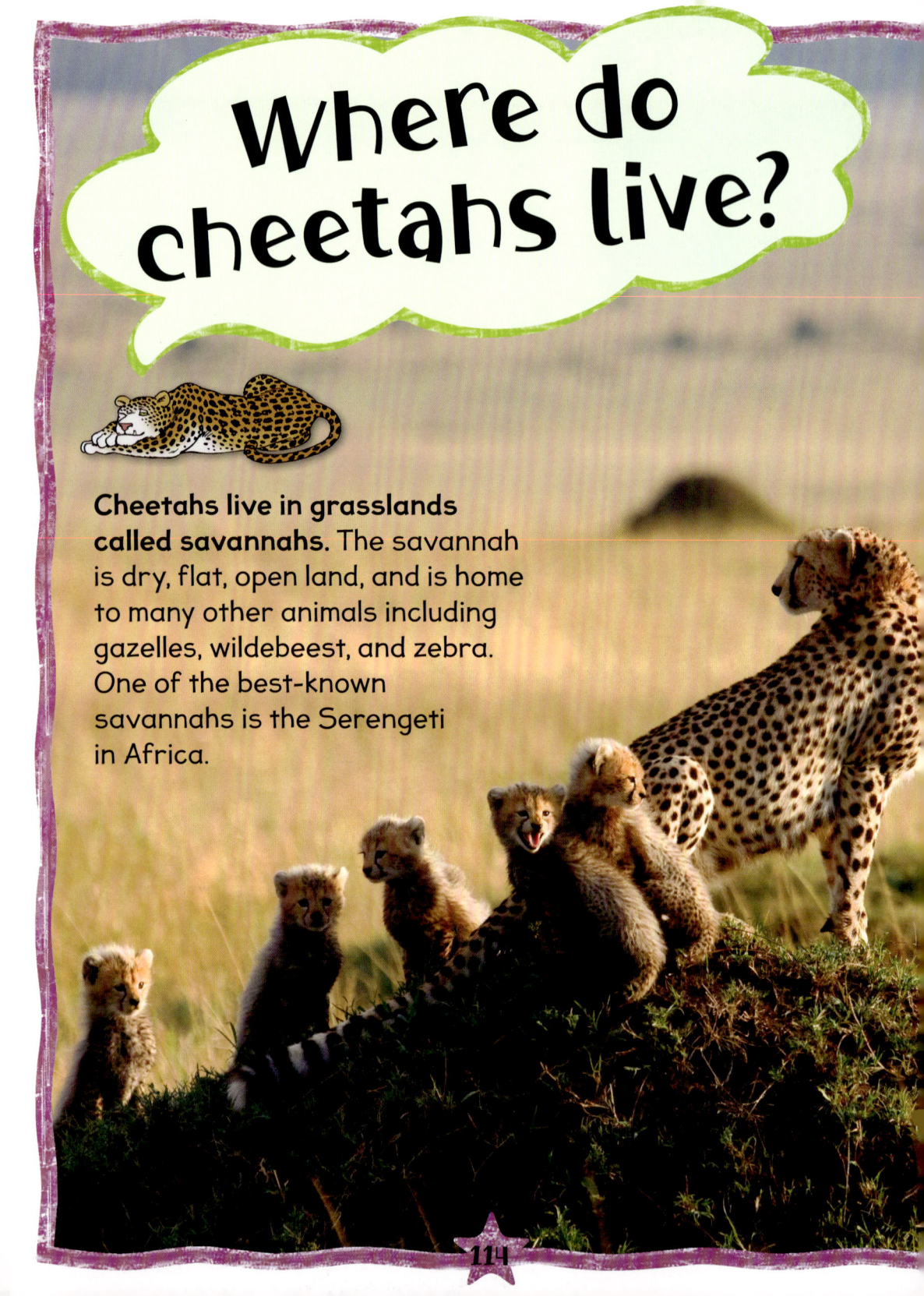

Cheetahs live in grasslands called savannahs. The savannah is dry, flat, open land, and is home to many other animals including gazelles, wildebeest, and zebra. One of the best-known savannahs is the Serengeti in Africa.

Why do cats wash their faces?

Cats wash their faces to spread their scent over their body. Cats have scent-producing body parts called glands on their chin. They use their paws to wipe the scent from their glands and when the cat walks, it can mark its area, or territory.

Play
With a friend, collect some pebbles and sticks and use them to mark out your own territories.

Lion

Slow down!
In the wild, cheetahs have a short life span. Their running speed gets a lot slower as they get older so they are less successful when they hunt.

How often do tigers eat?

Tigers can go more than one week without food. When tigers catch an animal they can eat 90 pounds of meat and don't need to eat again for eight or nine days!

How do snow leopards keep warm?

Snow leopards live on snowy mountains in Central Asia. To keep warm in winter they grow a thick coat of fur and store extra layers of fat under their skin. They also wrap their long tails around their bodies when they sleep to keep in heat.

Snow leopard

Which cat goes fishing?

The jaguar is an expert at fishing. Sometimes it waves its tail over the water to trick hungry fish before it strikes. Jaguars also fish for turtles and tortoises. Their jaws are so powerful that they can easily crack open a turtle shell.

Jaguar

Snowshoes!

Siberian tigers have large padded paws. They act as snowshoes and stop the tiger from sinking into the snow as it walks.

How do tigers stay cool?

Tigers such as the Bengal tiger live in places where it gets extremely hot in the summer. They can often be seen lying in pools of water to cool off, or resting in a shady area out of the hot sun.

Make

Paint a picture of your favorite big cat. Make it as colorful as you like and give your big cat a name.

Why do fawns have spots?

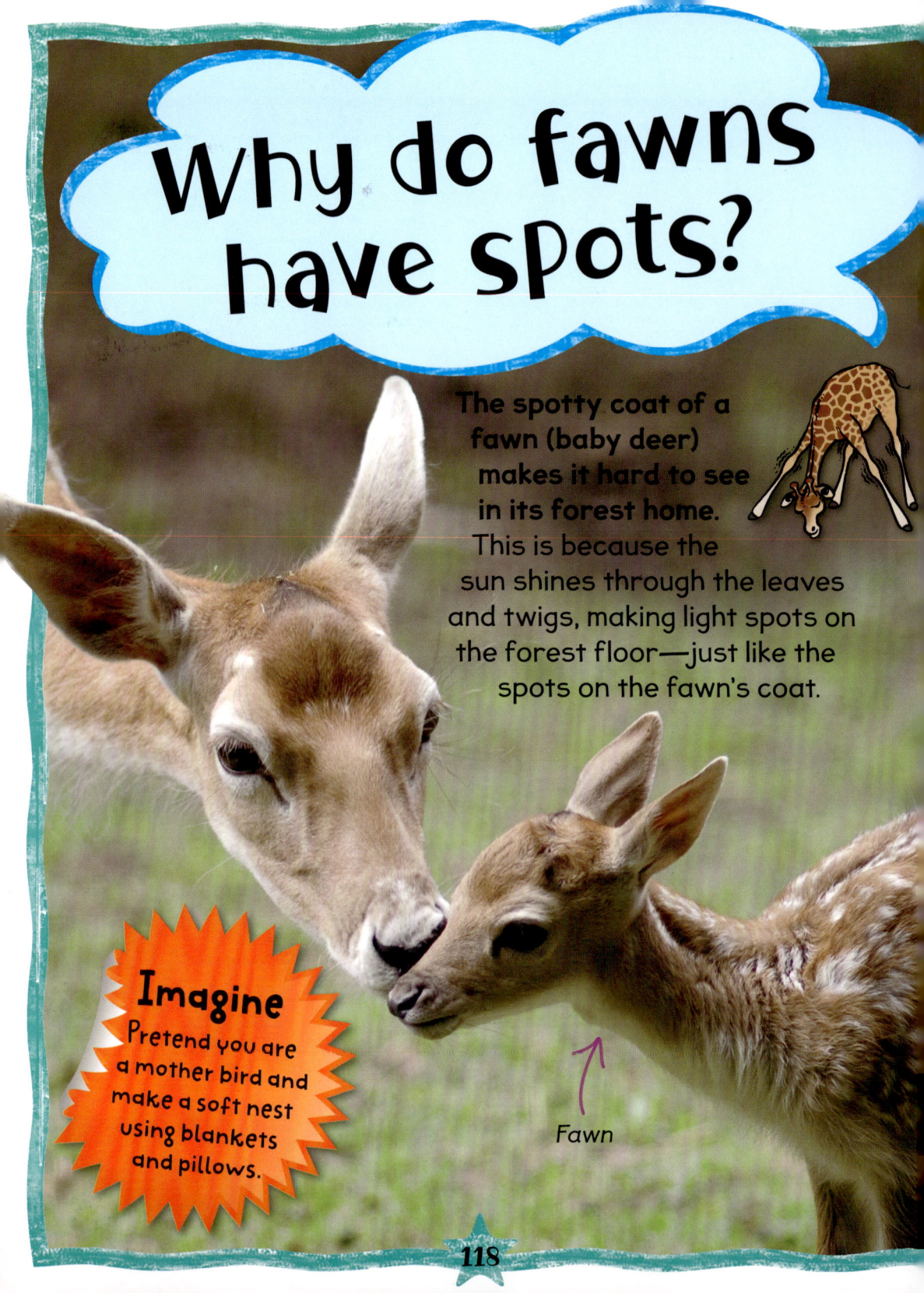

The spotty coat of a fawn (baby deer) makes it hard to see in its forest home. This is because the sun shines through the leaves and twigs, making light spots on the forest floor—just like the spots on the fawn's coat.

Imagine
Pretend you are a mother bird and make a soft nest using blankets and pillows.

Fawn

How do monkeys clean their babies?

Monkeys groom their young with their fingers and pick out bits of dead skin, insects, and dirt. Many animals also lick their babies to keep them clean.

Trunk call

Elephants use their trunks for many things, such as grabbing food from trees. Baby elephants have to learn to control their trunks.

Macaque monkey family

What do baby sharks eat?

Some eat other baby sharks! The eggs of the sand tiger shark hatch inside the mother's body. The first young to hatch then feed on the other eggs. When the sharks are born they are about 3 feet long.

Why do baby animals play?

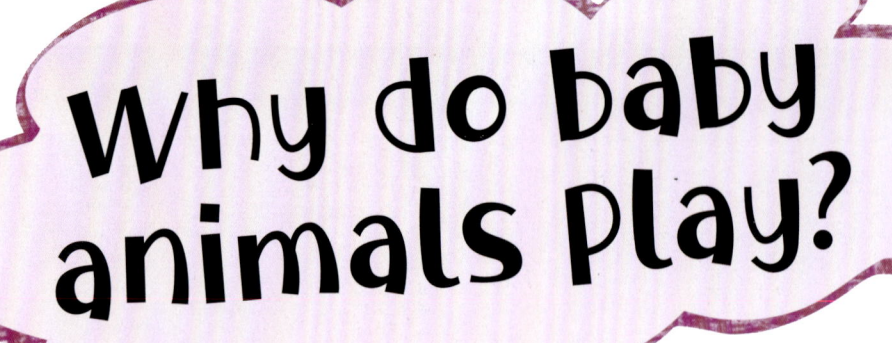

Lots of baby animals, such as otter pups, love to play. It helps them grow stronger and learn skills they will need as adults. Play fighting and chasing helps young animals learn how to hunt and catch prey.

Otter pups

Which bird makes the biggest nest?

The bald eagle makes the biggest nest of any bird. The largest ever seen was about 20 feet deep—big enough for a giraffe to hide in! The eagles use the same nest every year and add more sticks to it each time.

Bald eagle nest

Biggest egg
The ostrich lays the biggest egg of any bird. It weighs more than 3 pounds—that's the same as 24 hen's eggs!

Are baby snakes dangerous?

Some are. Not all types of snake use venom to kill their prey, but those that do, such as rattlesnakes, can give a deadly bite soon after they are born.

Ask
Find out how much you weighed at birth and measure out the same amount using weighing scales.

Where do baby rabbits live?

Baby rabbits are called kits and they live in a cozy nest called a burrow. The burrow is underground and lined with hay, straw, and fur to help keep the kits warm.

Burrow

Kits

When can foals walk?

Just a few hours after they are born! Foals need to be able to walk soon after birth, as they may have to escape from animals that hunt them. Foals also stay close to their moms for safety.

Foal

Greedy!

Caterpillars spend all their time eating and can grow to more than 30,000 times the size they were when they hatched!

Draw

What does your favorite baby animal look like? Draw a picture and color it in.

Do baby animals laugh?

Some do! Gorillas, chimps, and orangutans laugh when they're playing or tickling each other, just like we do. Scientists think that some other animals, such as dogs, may also laugh.

How do polar bear cubs keep warm?

Polar bear cubs

Polar bears live in the Arctic, where it is always very cold. The mother bear digs a den under the snow where her cubs are born. They live there until they are three months old. It is surprisingly warm and cosy in the den!

Play
Would you be a good mom or dad? Pretend your teddy bear is a baby and look after it carefully all day.

① Caterpillar hatches from its egg.

② Pupa is formed.

③ Butterfly breaks out of its pupa.

When do caterpillars become butterflies?

When a caterpillar has grown as big as it can, it stops eating and makes a hard case around itself called a pupa. Inside the pupa the caterpillar's body changes into a butterfly. The butterfly then breaks out of the pupa and flies away.

④ Butterfly flies away.

Big baby
Blue whales have the world's biggest babies. They are about 26 feet long at birth—that's roughly as long as two cars!

Why do scorpions carry their young?

Scorpions carry their babies on their backs until they are big and strong enough to take care of themselves. They climb onto their mom's back when they hatch and are carried around for the first two weeks.

Do baby elephants leave their herd?

Young elephants stay with their moms for many years. The males will eventually leave their close family groups and live alone or with other males, but females stay with their herd.

Calf

Make
Find and stick lots of pictures of baby animals to a big sheet of paper to make a poster.

Chick breaking out.

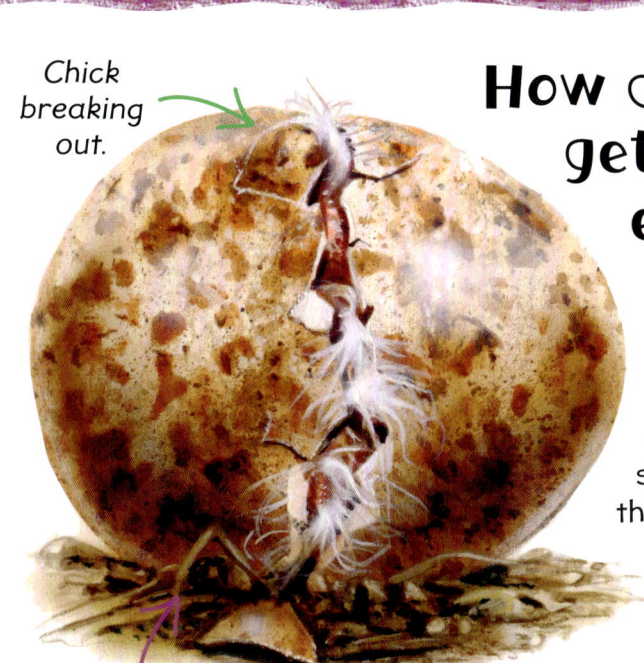

How does a chick get out of its egg?

A baby bird has a tiny spike, called an egg tooth, on its beak. When it is ready to hatch, the chick makes a little hole in the shell with the egg tooth and then struggles out.

Egg

Busy mom

Virginia opossums can have up to 13 babies at a time. The babies are tiny at birth and stay with their mom for about three months.

Do badgers keep their nests clean?

Yes they do. Badgers live in underground nests called setts, and use grass, leaves, and straw for bedding. The badgers bring their bedding out of the sett to air it and then throw out old, dirty bedding.

When do fox cubs leave their dens?

Fox cubs are born blind and helpless so they stay in their dens for the first few weeks. If their home is disturbed, the mother fox may move her cubs to a new den. Most cubs make their first outing when they are four weeks old.

Fox cubs

Why do cuckoos lay eggs quickly?

Because they lay their eggs in other birds' nests, instead of making their own. The other bird then looks after and feeds the cuckoo chick. A cuckoo lays an egg in just nine seconds—most birds take several minutes!

Clever baby

A gorilla baby develops more quickly than a human baby. They can crawl at about two months and walk at nine months.

Think

To be noticed, human babies cry. What noise do you think baby birds make to get attention?

Male hornbill feeding female.

Which bird has the safest nest?

The female hornbill makes her nest in a tree hole. The male then blocks up the hole with mud so that she and the eggs are safe from hunters. He leaves a hole for her beak so he can feed her while she's inside.

What is a primate?

Monkeys and apes are primates. They have big brains and are very clever. Most primates are furry. They have hands with thumbs and fingernails. Humans are primates too.

Spider monkeys

Cry baby!
Bush babies are noisy primates that live in forests. When they make loud calls to each other, they sound like crying babies.

Spell
How many words can you make using the letters in the word PRIMATE?

Are gorillas scary?

Gorillas are usually gentle animals. However they can be very fierce if they have to protect their families. Males can die fighting to save their young.

Do monkeys and apes have tails?

Monkeys have tails, but apes don't. Tails help monkeys to climb and keep their balance. Apes are usually larger than monkeys and they also have bigger brains. Gorillas, chimpanzees (chimps), bonobos, orangutans, gibbons, and humans are apes.

Orangutan

Why do chimps lick sticks?

Because the sticks get covered with juicy bugs! Chimps poke sticks into big termite nests. The insects swarm over the sticks, which the chimps then pull out so they can lick up the tasty termites.

Chimps

Sign
Use the Internet to discover how to sign for "drink" and "thank you."

Greedy monkey!
Barbary macaques have large cheek pouches. When they find food, they stuff it into their pouches and save it for later.

Do chimps like to chatter?

Some do! A chimp called Washoe learned how to use sign language to talk. She used her hands to make signs for lots of words, such as "drink" and "food."

Squirrel monkey

Why do monkeys sleep in trees?

Monkeys will hide among tree branches as it is safer to be up high than on the ground. Animals that want to eat other animals are called predators. The predators of squirrel monkeys include eagles, baboons, and porcupines.

Do apes make good moms?

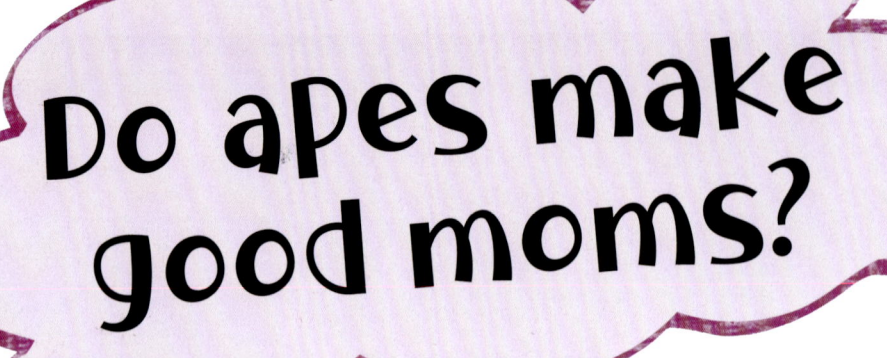

Yes—apes are good moms and look after their babies. Orangutan babies need their moms the most of all apes, staying with them until they are about eight years old. That's longer than any other primate, apart from humans.

Orangutan and baby

Why does an aye-aye have a long finger?

An aye-aye has a long finger to get to tasty grubs. These little primates tap trees with their fingers. If they hear a grub moving inside, they make a hole and pull it out with their extra-long middle finger.

Aye-aye

What a racket!

Some mangabeys make a "honk-bark" noise. Others "whoop" to call each other and make a "gobble" sound to say who they are.

Why do orangutans climb trees?

Orangutans climb trees to play among the branches, to find fruit to eat, and to stay safe. Predators such as tigers, leopards, and crocodiles hunt orangutans.

Make

Who looks after you? Create them a beautiful card to say "thank you."

Why do chimps kiss?

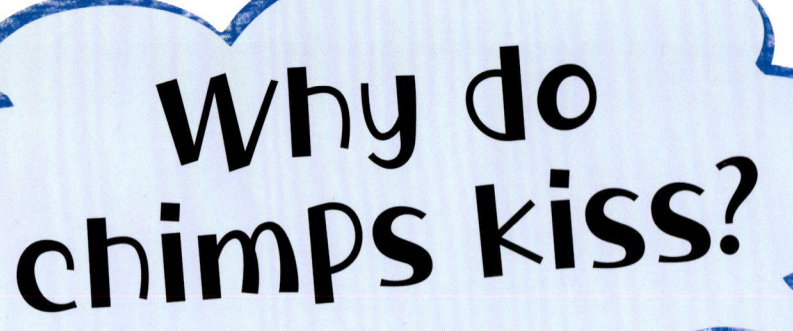

Chimps can be very loving to members of their family. They like to sit together and kiss, stroke, and groom each other. If chimps are annoyed they cough, but if they are angry they bark, cry, and scream.

Chimps

Do primates use tools?

Some primates use tools to help them get food. Capuchin monkeys use heavy rocks to crack open hard nuts. Apes can use tools too. They even teach each other how to use rocks to open nuts.

Brown capuchin

Keeping warm!
Japanese macaques live in mountainous areas. Some keep warm by soaking in pools of hot water that bubble up from the ground.

Discover
Use books and the Internet to find other animals that use tools.

When do baboons show off?

Male baboons love to show off when there are females about. They swagger around to show off their big muscles, long fangs, and fine fur.

How fast can a gibbon swing?

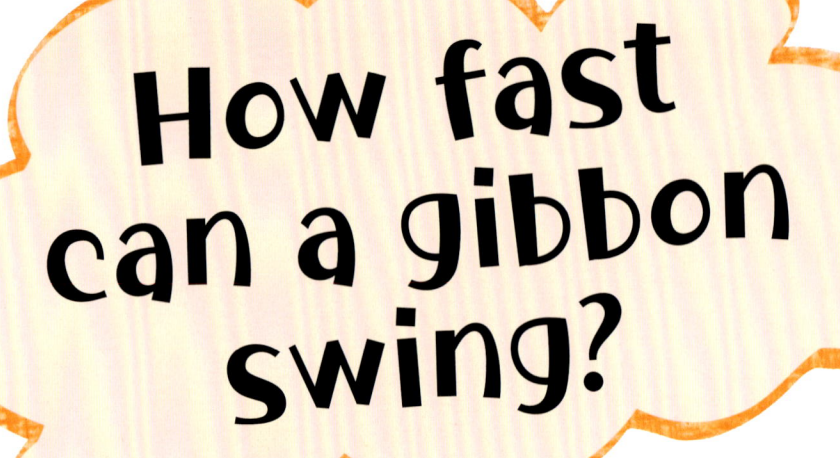

Gibbons move faster than any other primate. They can swing through trees at great speed—up to 35 miles an hour. Gibbons can cover up to 50 feet in just one swing.

Gibbons

Crab-eating macaque

Do monkeys eat crabs?

Some monkeys will eat almost anything they can find! Crab-eating macaques live in swamps and they will grab crabs and frogs out of shallow water. Sometimes they just drop into the cool water for a swim.

Do primates have hands and feet like us?

Instead of paws and claws, primates have fingers, toes, and flat fingernails just like us. This means they can grab hold of branches and delicately pinch small things.

Count
If one macaque can catch five crabs, how many can three macaques catch?

Super movers!
Spider monkeys are some of the fastest primate climbers. They have very long arms, legs, and tails.

Do monkeys change color?

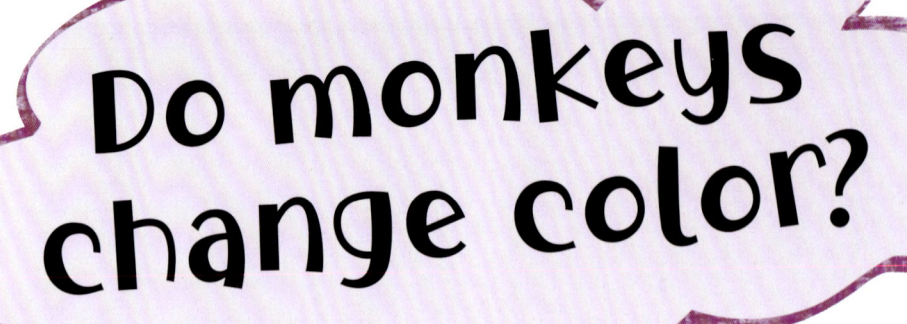

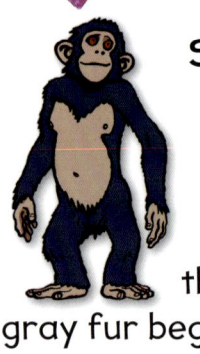

Silvered langurs do! These monkeys have silver-gray fur, but their babies are born bright orange. After three months, gray fur begins to grow. No one knows why the babies are orange—perhaps it reminds the older monkeys to be gentle with them.

Silvered langur

Silvered langur baby

Which ape has a colorful bottom?

A healthy male mandrill baboon has a brightly colored bottom. Their bald bottoms have blue, pink, or lilac skin. Female baboons often have pink or bright red bottoms.

A handy tail!
Monkeys use their tails like an extra arm or leg. They can hang from branches using their tails.

Sifaka

Why does a sifaka skip?

Skipping is a fast way for sifakas (a type of lemur) to travel. They stand upright, with their arms stretched out, and skip sideways, scooting across the ground. Sifakas stick their tails out so they don't fall over as they hop, bound, and leap.

Imagine
Pretend to be a sifaka and skip about!

How big is a gorilla?

Adult male gorillas are very big. They are called silverbacks, and they are up to 70 inches in height and weigh about 650 pounds. That's the same weight as almost four people!

Silverback gorilla

Measure
Use a measuring tape to find out how tall a gorilla is.

What is the ugliest monkey?

Red uakaris (say: wak-ar-ees) are one of the ugliest monkeys. When they are born, baby uakaris have gray faces, but they turn bright red as they get older.

Bathtime fun!

Suryia the orangutan lives in a wildlife park. He loved splashing in the bath and was taken to a pool. Suryia can now swim underwater!

Red uakari

Why do gorillas beat their chests?

When a silverback gorilla stands up and beats his chest, it is time to get away fast! This is his way of warning you that he is getting angry and might attack.

Why do hippos attack each other?

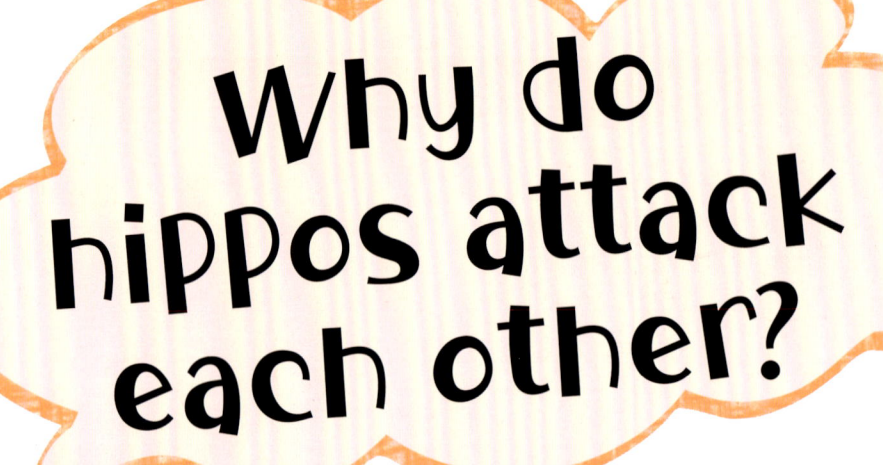

Male hippos attack each other to defend the patch of land where they live. When they fight, hippos stand face-to-face with their mouths wide-open and swipe at each other with their tusklike teeth. Sometimes these fights end in the death of one or even both hippos.

Hippos

144

Which bird can kill while it flies?

Lots of birds hunt "on the wing." The peregrine falcon is the fastest hunting animal in the world and dives at 140 miles an hour. It chases its prey before attacking it to tire it out.

Peregrine falcon

Hold it, hippopotamus!
Hippos and whales are closely related—maybe this is why hippos can hold their breath underwater for 12 minutes!

Do army ants go hunting?

Army ants hunt in groups, sometimes of more than one million ants. They move forward in a wave across the ground. Ants at the front of the group kill insects and small lizards in their path, while ants further back carry food to the nest.

Army ants

Explore
Ants live in most places, even in your garden. Take a look outside and see if you can spot any.

Why do snakes have fangs?

Poisonous snakes such as rattlesnakes have an extra-long pair of teeth called fangs. A deadly poison called venom runs along a groove in each fang. When the snake bites an animal, its fangs sink into the animal's skin and venom is injected.

Rattlesnake

Which creature kills with its tail?

All scorpions have a poisonous sting in their tail. They use their front clawlike arms to hold their prey, while their tail-sting injects a harmful venom. Few scorpions can badly injure a human, but a sting from the death stalker scorpion can kill.

Common yellow scorpion

Death match!

Scorpions normally live alone because most of them eat other scorpions. If two scorpions meet, they will fight to the death and the loser is eaten by the winner.

Why are eels shocking?

Electric eels use electricity to zap their prey and to attack other animals that threaten them. The electric eel, which is actually a type of fish, can produce up to 600 volts of electricity—enough to kill a human!

Discover

Some eels use electricity to hunt. What things in your home use electricity?

Why do crocodiles have big teeth?

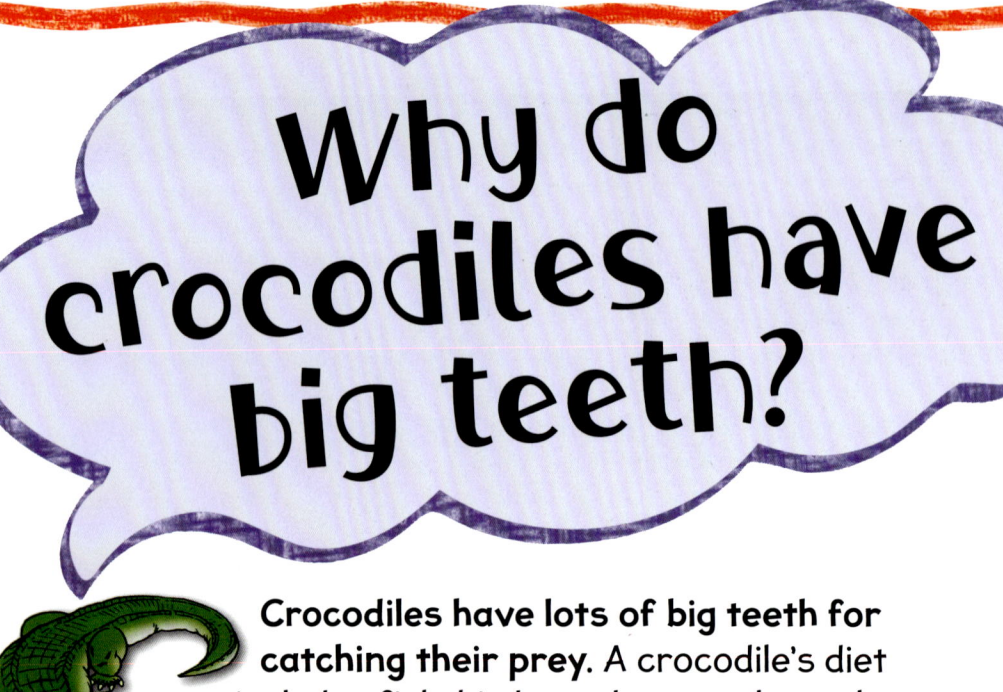

Crocodiles have lots of big teeth for catching their prey. A crocodile's diet includes fish, birds, and mammals, such as gazelle and wildebeest. The crocodile's sharp teeth and powerful jaws help it to keep hold of its prey and to bite chunks off to swallow.

Nile crocodile

Do snakes eat people?

Pythons, such as Burmese pythons, have been known to attack and kill humans—but rarely. These snakes usually eat small mammals and birds, but can open their mouths wide enough to swallow animals such as pigs and deer whole!

Burmese python

Boiled eggs!
Whether a baby crocodile is a female or a male depends on temperature. A female will develop in a warm egg and a male will develop in a cool egg.

Make
Using an old sock for the body, buttons for eyes, and wooden pegs for teeth, make a crocodile hand puppet.

Gazelle

What is a deathspin?

A deathspin is what crocodiles and alligators do to drown their prey. A crocodile pulls its victim underwater and twists and turns until the animal is dead. The crocodiles' strong jaws keep a grip on the animal as it rolls and turns in the water.

What is a black widow?

The black widow is one of the world's most deadly spiders. Black widows only bite if they are disturbed. Male black widows are harmless, but a bite from a female can kill a human. Sometimes, the female black widow eats the male after mating.

Black widow

Think
Lots of people are scared of spiders. Are there any creepy-crawlies that you are afraid of?

Why do wolves snarl?

Wolves snarl when they are angry or threatened by another animal. When a wolf snarls, its lips curl back to show its long, sharp teeth and its nostrils widen. The fur on the wolf's back also stands on end to make it look bigger to an attacker.

Wolf

Scary sound!

A wolf's growl is a very low, deep sound. They growl to threaten other wolves and to show they have power over a group of wolves, which is called a pack.

Why do crocodiles eat rotting meat?

Crocodiles eat rotting meat because it is easier to swallow. Crocodiles and alligators store their food by wedging the dead animal under an underwater branch or log, so that it rots down. Sometimes, they store their food for several weeks.

What is the deadliest lizard?

The Komodo dragon is the deadliest, and biggest, meat-eating lizard. It eats every part of an animal, including its bones. This lizard has a poisonous bite, so even if prey escapes, the Komodo dragon just follows it until it weakens and dies.

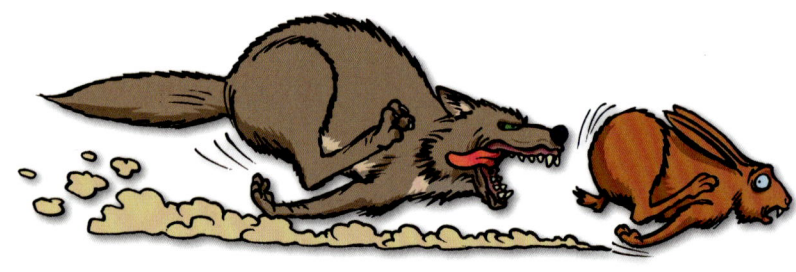

Komodo dragon

How do coyotes catch their prey?

Coyotes are fast runners and often chase speedy jackrabbits across rocks and up hills. When hunting larger animals such as deer, a group of coyotes chase the animal to tire it and bite its neck to stop it breathing.

Anaconda

Look
Snakes open their mouths very wide to eat big animals. How wide can you open yours?

Why do snakes squeeze their prey?

Some snakes, such as anacondas, squeeze their prey to death instead of using poison. These snakes are called constrictors. The captured animal is squeezed tighter and tighter until it can't breathe. Then the snake swallows it whole!

Deadly down under!
Australia has more poisonous snakes for its size than any other country—including eight of the world's ten deadliest snakes.

Which owl hunts other owls?

The eagle owl does. Eagle owls hunt "on the wing" (while flying) for any kind of bird, including other owls. As well as hunting in the air, these owls hunt on the ground for insects, reptiles, and mammals. The eagle owl is the biggest owl.

Eagle owl

What do fleas eat?

Fleas live on most furry animals, and sometimes humans. They jump from animal to animal feeding on blood and can spread disease. Fleas were responsible for spreading the Black Death, a disease that killed millions of people in the 14th century.

Flea

What is the deadliest octopus?

The blue-ringed octopus is the world's most dangerous octopus—and it's only 4 to 8 inches long. It grabs prey with its sticky tentacles and then gives a bite that injects venom. Its venom is strong enough to kill a human in four minutes!

Blue-ringed octopus

Silent hunter!

An owl's feathers have fluffy edges. This softens the sound of their wings flapping so they can swoop down on their prey in silence.

Count

An octopus has eight tentacles. How many tentacles would three octopuses have?

Index

A
agoutis 97
aircraft 11
algae 46
alligators 149, 151
anacondas 153
Antarctica 42, 55
ants 99, 145
apes 130, 131, 134, 135, 137
Arctic 33, 58, 124
army ants 145
astronauts 33
avalanches 43
aye-ayes 135

B
babies, animal 75, 118–129, 134, 140, 149
baboons 133, 137, 141
badgers 127
bald eagles 121
bananas 77
Barbary macaques 133
barnacles 52, 62
bats 79
batteries 11, 15
Bay of Fundy 69
bays 66
beachcombing 69
beaches, sandy 63, 67
bears
  polar bears 58, 61, 124
  sun bears 101
bees 78, 101
beetles 65, 96
Bengal tigers 117
bicycles 7
big cats 106–117
birds 71, 79, 81, 89, 91, 92, 102, 121, 127, 145, 154
  eggs 129
  flightless 97
  seabirds 59, 64, 65, 69, 75
Black Death 155
black widows 150
blood 26, 27
blood cells 21, 27
blood-suckers 93, 155
blue whales 53, 125
blue-ringed octopuses 155
bones 20–21
bonobos 131
Boyd's dragons 100
brain waves 29
brains 23, 28–29, 130, 131
breathing 24–25
Burmese pythons 149
burning 8–9
burrows 122
bush babies 130
butterflies 82, 84, 98, 125

C
cables 14
cacao beans 95
cacti 81, 85
camouflage 101, 103, 110, 118
candles 9
capuchin monkeys 137
cars 7
cassowaries 97
caterpillars 83, 99, 123, 125
cell phones 17
cells 19, 21, 27, 29
cerebellum 28, 29
cerebrum 28
cheetahs 114, 115
chemicals 8
chicks 59, 65, 127
chimpanzees (chimps) 123, 131, 132–133, 136
chocolate 95
Christmas Island red crabs 73
circuits 15
cirrus clouds 41
cleaner wrasses 51
cliffs 67
clouded leopards 111
clouds 40, 41
clown fish 50, 51
collarbone 20
compasses 34
computers 16–17
constrictors (snakes) 104, 153
coral reefs 50–51, 70
core, Earth's 34, 35
coyotes 152
crab-eating macaques 139
crabeater seals 61
crabs 47, 57, 68, 73
craters 30
crocodiles 56, 135, 148, 149, 151
crust, Earth's 34, 38
cubs 107, 124, 128
cuckoos 129
cumulus clouds 41

D
day and night 32, 33
deathspin 149
deer 118
deltas 67
dens 124, 128
dermis 19
deserts 81
dinosaurs 77
diseases 155
doctors 29
dogs 123
dolphins 49
dugongs 73

E

eagle owls 154
eagles 102, 121, 133
ears 11, 21
Earth
  day and night 32, 33
  formation 30
  layers 34–35
  magnetic field 13
  spinning 32–33, 61
earthquakes 35, 38–39, 63
EEG machines 29
eels 51, 147
egg tooth 127
eggs
  birds 59, 121, 127, 129
  crabs 73
  crocodiles 149
  fish 119
  insects 65
  turtles 74
electric eels 147
electric motors 11
electricity 11, 12, 14–15, 29
electricity pylons 14
electromagnets 12
elephants 105, 119, 126
email 16
emerald tree boas 104
emperor penguins 59
endangered animals 111
energy 8
epicenter 38
epidermis 19
extinction 111

F

fairy penguins 59
fall 86
fangs 146
fawns 118
fighting (animals) 131, 144, 147
fingernails 130, 139
fireflies 101
fireworks 8
fish 48–49, 51, 71, 97
flamingos 71
fleas 155
flies 88
flowers 76, 78, 82, 84, 85
foals 123
forces 6, 7
foxes 69, 128
freshwater 45
friction 6
frogs 99, 103
frost 87
frowning 23
fulmars 65
fungi 83
fur 107, 116, 137, 140, 151

G

gazelles 114, 148
geckos 91, 105
gentoo penguins 59
germs 18, 27
gibbons 131, 138
glands 115
glow-worms 101
golden poison arrow frogs 99
Goliath spiders 93
gorillas 103, 123, 129, 131, 142, 143
grasslands 113, 114
gravity 7
Great Barrier Reef 51
great white sharks 48
grooming 119, 136
groupers 51
gum trees 89

H

habitats 90
headlands 66
heart 23, 26–27
heartbeats 26
Hercules beetles 96
herds 126
herring 49
hippos 144, 145
hornbills 129
horses 123
howler monkeys 95
human body 18–29
humans 130, 131
hummingbirds 81
humpback whales 52
hunting 109, 120, 145, 154

I

Iberian lynx 111
ice 42
iguanas 57, 75
Internet 16–17
intertidal zone 63, 71
iron 12, 34
islands 45

J

jaguars 117
Japanese macaques 137
jellyfish 57
jet engines 11
joints 21, 22

K

kidneys 27
killer whales 49
kits (baby rabbits) 122
koalas 89
Komodo dragons 152–153
krill 53

L

lagoons 70, 71
larynx 25
laughing 123
lava 37, 45
leaf insects 101
leaflitter toads 103
leatherback turtles 57
leaves 76, 86, 99
leeches 93
lemurs 99, 102, 141
leopard seals 55

leopards 111, 112, 116, 135
levers 6
light 10
light bulbs 15
light rays 10
lightning 15
limpets 46, 62
lionfish 51
lions 107, 108–109, 115
lizards 57, 75, 91, 100, 105, 152
lobsters 57
lugworms 68
lungs 24, 25, 26
lynx 111

M

macaques 133, 137, 139
macaws 91
machines 6–7, 14
magma 36
magnetic fields 13
magnetic poles 13
magnets 11, 12–13, 34
manatees 73
mandrills 141
mangabeys 105, 135
mangroves 65, 72
mantle, Earth's 34
marrow 21
mating 150
meteorites 30
millipedes 99
modems 16
monkeys 95, 105, 119, 130, 131, 133, 137, 139, 140, 141, 143
Moon 30, 31, 33, 61
moray eels 51
moths 84
mountains 35, 37, 41, 43, 45
mudskippers 71
muscle fibers 22
muscles 22–23, 25, 26, 29
mushrooms 83
mussels 62

N

nails 130, 139
narwhals 53
nectar 81, 82, 84
nerves 19, 22, 23, 29
nests 121, 129
night *see* day and night
Nile crocodiles 148
North and South Poles 61
nutcrackers 79
nuts 79, 97, 137

O

oceans and seas 31, 33, 40, 44–45
ocelots 111
octopuses 155
okapis 103
opossums 127
orangutans 103, 123, 131, 134, 135, 143
orcas 49
ostriches 121
otters 55, 69, 120
owls 154, 155
oxygen 24, 26, 27

P

packs (animals) 151
paperbark trees 87
parrotfish 50
parrots 91
pebbles 67
penguins 59, 61
peregrine falcons 145
Philippine eagles 102
piranhas 97
pivots 6
planets 30
plants 76–89
  desert plants 81
  flowers 76, 78, 82, 84, 85
  plant parts 76
  seeds 82, 83, 87, 89
plates, Earth's 35, 37

playground rides 6
playing 29, 120
poison arrow frogs 99
poisonous animals
  frogs 99
  lizards 152
  octopuses 155
  scorpions 147
  snakes 121, 146, 153
  spiders 150
polar bears 58, 61, 124
poles, magnetic 13
pollen 78, 79, 82
polyps (coral) 50
porcupines 133
potatoes 85
potoos 91
power plants 14
prides 108
primates 130–143
prisms 10
puffins 64, 75
pumas 109, 113
pupae 125
pups, sharks 49
pushes and pulls 7
pythons 149

Q R

Queen Alexandra's bird-wing butterflies 98
rabbits 111, 113, 122
rafflesias 85
rain 40–41, 42, 81, 93
rainbows 10
rain forests 85, 90–105, 113
ramps 7
rare animals 103
rattlesnakes 121, 146
razor shells 68
red uakaris 143
redwoods, giant 80
reserves, animal 113
Richter Scale 39
ring-tailed lemurs 99

rivers 40
rock pools 46–47
rocks 13, 30, 31
roller coasters 7
roots 72, 76, 87, 89,

S
saltwater crocodiles 56
sand 67, 68
sand dunes 65
sand tiger sharks 49, 119
savannahs 114
scent-marking 115
scorpions 125, 147
sea anemones 46, 47, 71
sea cows 73
sea lions 49, 54
sea otters 55
sea snakes 57
seabirds 59, 64, 65, 69, 75
seahorses 50
seals 48, 54, 55, 61
seashells 46, 62
seashores 60–75
seesaws 6
seedlings 79
seeds 82, 83, 87, 89
sensors 18, 19
Serengeti, Africa 114
setts 127
sharks 48–49, 119
shingle 66
shrimps 68
Siberian tigers 106, 107, 117
sifakas 141
silverback gorillas 142, 143
silvered langurs 140
singing 25, 52, 55
skateboards 18, 19
skeleton 20–21
skin 18–19
skipping 141
sloths 94
slugs 99
smiling 23
snails 99

snakes 57, 104, 121, 146, 149, 153
snow 42–43
snow leopards 116
snowflakes 42
sockets 14, 15
soil 89
sounds 11
speaking 29
spider monkeys 130, 139
spiders 93, 150
spits 66
sponges 47
squirrel monkeys 133
stacks 66
starfish 46, 57
static electricity 15
steel 12
stems 76, 79
stings 147
strandline 69
stratus clouds 41
Sun 30, 79, 81
sun bears 101
sunlight 10
sweat 19

T
tails 131, 141
tapirs 95
teeth
  animal 97, 105, 148, 151
  egg tooth 127
  fangs 146
  tusks 53, 105
temperatures 9, 42
tentacles 71, 155
termites 132
territories 115
thermometers 9
thinking 29
thresher sharks 49
thunderstorms 15
tides 46, 61, 68, 69
tiger beetles 65
tiger sharks 49

tigers 65, 103, 106–107, 110, 111, 115, 117, 135
toads 69, 103
toadstools 83
toilet 27
tokay geckos 91
tongues, animal 84, 103
tool use, animal 132, 137
tortoises 117
toucans 92
touch 18, 19, 29
trains 7
trees 72, 80, 86, 87, 112, 135
trenches 45
trunks (elephants) 119
tsunamis 63
turtles 57, 74–75, 117
tusks 53, 105

U V
urine 27
venom 121, 147, 155
Venus flytraps 88
voice box 25
volcanoes 35, 36, 37, 45

W Z
walruses 54, 55
waste, bodily 27
water cycle 40
water vapor 40
waves 63, 67
whales 52–53, 125, 145
wheelbarrows 7
wheels 7
white light 10
wild cats 73
wildebeest 114, 148
windpipe 24
winds 61, 63
wolves 151
World Wide Web 16–17
worms 89
zebras 114

Acknowledgments

All artworks are from the Miles Kelly Artwork Bank
The publishers would like to thank the following sources for the use of their photographs.
(t = top, b = bottom, l = left, r = right, c = center, bg = background)

Dreamstime 145(tl) Suerob

FLPA 137(tr) Pete Oxford/Minden Pictures

Fotolia 70(b) Vladimir Ovchinnikov; 74(cl) SLDigi; 86(b) Giovanni Catalani

ShutterstockPremier 6(b) Sergey Lavrentev; 7(tr) Jorge Salcedo, (b) Bertl123; 8(bg) Wade H. Massie; 9(tr) Ruth Black, (bl) Serhiy Shullye; 10(bg) XYZ; 12(bg) takasu; 14(bg) ThomBal; 16(bg) Anton Balazh; 18(bg) Tomasz Trojanowski; 20(cl) Ralf Juergen Kraft; 22(bg) Frederick R. Matzen; 23(br) Jaren Jai Wicklund; 25(tr) SpeedKingz; 27(br) abhijith3747; 29(tr) beerkoff; 34(bg) Mopic; 35(tr) beboy, (bc) Bjartur Snorrason; 37(tr) Galyna Andrushko; 39(cl) Menna, (c) Joseph Sohm, (cr) Yankane; 41(tc) Serg64, (tr) Patryk Kosmider, (cr) Sergey Sergeev; 42(bg) Jan Martin Will; 43(bg) Maygutyak; 44(b) ktsdesign; 47(cr) Damsea; 52(bg) Achimdiver; 54(b) Mariusz Potocki; 55(tl) Marcos Amend; 56(b) Meister Photos, (tc) Neil Burton; 58(b) Fotokon; 59(tl) ChameleonsEye; 60(bg) Roxana Gonzalez; 61(t) Photodynamic; 72(b) Niar; 79(tl) Anest; 80(l) Urosr; 82(bg) artjazz; 89(b) Daniel Hebert; 90–91(bg) Juriah Mosin; 92(bg) Eduardo Rivero; 94(bg), 99(tl), 101(tr) & 108–109(bg) Eric Isselee; 95(tr) Dr Morley Read; 105(t) Sergey Uryadnikov; 110(bg) olga_gl; 111(t) llaszlo; 112(b) Ewan Chesser; 113(t) & 116(bg) Dennis W Donohue; 114(bg) Gail Johnson; 115(tr) Leksele; 118(bc) ehtesham; 119(cl) tratong; 121(tr) Kane513; 126(bg) Ekkachai; 131(br) javarman; 133(br) Sara Robinson; 134(b) Eric Gevaert; 141(br) Bob Ascott; 142(bg) Mike Price; 146(b) Maria Dryfhout; 147(tr) EcoPrint; 149(tr) Fivespots; 151(tr) Tom Tietz

All other photographs are from: Digital Stock, digitalvision, Photodisc

Every effort has been made to acknowledge the source and copyright holder of each picture. Miles Kelly Publishing apologizes for any unintentional errors or omissions.